Building
an Effective
Youth Ministry

Creative Leadership Series

Building
an Effective
Youth Ministry

Glenn E. Ludwig

Creative Leadership Series
Lyle E. Schaller, Editor

Abingdon Press/Nashville

BUILDING AN EFFECTIVE YOUTH MINISTRY
Copyright © 1979 by Abingdon

Sixth Printing 1983

Library of Congress Cataloging in Publication Data

LUDWIG, GLENN E. 1946–
    Building an effective youth ministry.
    (Creative leadership series)
    Bibliography: p. 120
    1. Church work with youth—Lutheran Church.
    I. Title. II. Series.
    BV4447.L825   268'.433   79-12282

ISBN 0-687-03992-4

Scripture quotations noted TEV are from the Bible in
Today's English Version. Copyright © American Bible
Society 1966, 1971, 1976.

MANUFACTURED BY THE PARTHENON PRESS AT
NASHVILLE, TENNESSEE, UNITED STATES OF AMERICA

TO BETH,
    —whose partnership in ministry fills the
    pages of our past with exciting memories
    —and whose partnership in marriage has
    taught me the meaning of love

Foreword

In September of 1979 the number of children entering first grade was down by 1.1 million from the peak of 4.2 million first-graders in 1967–68. The impact of the "baby bust" of the late 1960s and early 1970s is being felt in Sunday schools all across the North American continent. During the 1980s the impact of the birth dearth will be felt in youth programs. The number of seventeen-year-olds will drop from a peak of over 4.2 million in 1978 to approximately 3.2 million in 1990. For every four teen-agers now available for a church's youth program there will be only three in 1990. This will make youth ministries one of the most competitive areas of programming as a growing number of congregations compete for a decreasing number of teen-agers.

How will creative church leaders respond?

In some congregations the response to a dying youth program will be: "Let's have a party and invite all the high-school kids. When we get them together, we can ask them what they want to do, and maybe we can build a new youth group in response to what they tell us." In the first chapter of this book Glenn Ludwig explains why that is the wrong question at the wrong time.

Perhaps the second most common response in the churches to the adult anxiety produced by the lack of a strong, vigorous, attractive, and growing youth program is, "Let's hire someone to be our youth director and have that person build the program" or "Let's find a young minister who can relate to the young people and make that the new minister's top priority." In the sixth chapter the author explains why this is not the appropriate beginning point. This point is underscored symbolically by making "The Big Kids—The Youth Advisors" chapter 6, not an earlier chapter. The staffing of a youth program, whether it be with lay volunteers or with a paid staff member, should be seen as part of a means to an end, not as the end in itself. Pastor Ludwig makes this point very clear by scheduling this chapter for the second half of the volume.

More important, it is impossible to make a wise and creative decision on staffing youth ministries until *after* decisions have been made on the theological assumptions that undergird the concept of a specialized ministry with youth, until *after* an effort has been made to understand the youth of today (they are not carbon copies of the youth of the 1960s!), and until *after* widespread agreement has been reached on structure and on the style of programming. These four issues are discussed in the second, third, fourth, and fifth chapters of this volume. After the congregational leaders have responded to these concerns, it is appropriate to begin discussing alternatives in staffing.

In other words, one of the most creative responses available to adult leaders in the churches as they ponder what to do about youth ministries is to read the first six chapters of this book *before* they begin to discuss how to delegate responsibility for implementation of a program to a lay couple or to a committee or to a paid staff member.

These first six chapters also are directed, of course, at the leaders, both lay and clergy, who have the direct responsibilities for the planning and the oversight of youth ministries. The final three chapters are directed at this audience in particular.

All eight of the volumes in the Creative Leadership Series published to date have been based on the assumption that creative and open-minded congregational leaders are seeking guidance as they respond to the challenges of the last quarter of the twentieth century. This means an active, not a passive, stance. *Leaders lead; they initiate!* Whether it be in seeking and welcoming a new pastor, a process described by Robert Graham Kemper in an earlier volume in this series; in assimilating new members; in managing the network of lay volunteers; in enhancing a sense of stewardship; or in planning for youth ministries, leaders must lead. The creative and open-minded church leader will find this volume by Glenn Ludwig to be a stimulating guidebook in planning for ministry with youth during the 1980s.

Lyle E. Schaller
Yokefellow Institute
Richmond, Indiana

Contents

Introduction

The purpose of this book is to provide a solid theoretical basis from which youth ministry can be built. It is not a cookbook which gives 101 recipes on "how to" form a youth group. Neither is it a workbook or manual with designs and directions on what to glue to what to have the pieces look like a youth group. Those kinds of books are important and useful; however, this book goes deeper.

It begins by asking the question, Why youth ministry? The attempt here is to understand the purpose for youth ministry by developing a theological and theoretical frame of reference. It is out of this framework, then, that issues such as the structure of a youth group, choice of programming, and the role of youth advisors are explored.

There are no easy answers in creative youth ministry, just some perceptive questions. This book asks those questions. It is my contention that as one understands theory, one then is able to create. An airplane, even though it looks like an airplane, will not fly unless its designer understands the theory of aerodynamics. It is no different in creating a solid youth ministry. It literally will not fly unless someone learns about theory.

Another bias is present throughout the book, and that is that youth ministry does not just happen. It takes a lot of hard work, a touch of creativity, and a large measure of openness. This is no recipe; it is fact. Throughout the book theories and ideas will be exchanged, but they are only as good as those who are willing to struggle with them. There are no easy

15

answers to developing a youth group that is alive and relevant.

A further contention of this book is that the theories and ideas related here are pertinent to youth ministry of various shapes and forms. From a group just forming, to an established youth ministry of many years, the book can help one in thinking through many issues that concern youth groups. The size or location of the group is also unimportant, because the issues of organizational structure, programming, advisors, and what to do are the same for all who are involved in youth ministry.

A word needs to be said about the terms "youth group" or "youth ministry." This refers to the organized, intentional ministry of any congregation that is directed *for, with,* and *by* the youth. When referring to youth, I am addressing young people of junior- and senior-high grades with an age span of twelve to nineteen years. Recognizing that some youth ministry is directed to younger grades and ages, I have primarily directed the ideas and theories of this book to the junior-senior-high youth group.

I am a practicing parish pastor who has worked in youth ministry since I was a youth-group participant. Beyond high school, I have served as an advisor to three different groups in three different churches. The applied theories of this book have been formulated and tested in working with churches large, small, and in-between, in rural and urban settings, with new groups just starting and with groups that have been going for a number of years. Over the past five years, my wife and I have served as parish consultants to congregations in youth ministry, led numerous workshops in youth ministry, served as program consultants on a synodical level, and coordinated a number of large youth gatherings, as well as developed a solid congregational youth ministry in the parishes where we have served. I am now serving as Chairman of the Board of Directors of Lutheran Youth Encounter, an independent, nonprofit corporation that provides relational youth ministry resources nationally. Therefore, the theory in this book is undergirded by real life examples. It is not theory developed in a vacuum, but theory formulated, tested, and successfully used.

There is a need for this type of book. There are numerous cookbooks and manuals on the market, but very little on solid theory. The book is written for those who work in youth ministry and who strive to be creative, namely lay volunteers (or youth advisors), pastors interested in youth ministry, seminarians, and the youth who are the identified leaders in a church. These youth workers need to know why they are doing what they are doing and how to create something meaningful in their programs. When they understand something of the whys, the cookbooks and manuals become useful resources in their creative processes.

Obviously, there are many significant persons involved in the preparation of any book. This one is no exception. Lyle Schaller shares my convictions, and this book is the result of his constant threats and encouragements to write. Beth Ludwig, an English teacher and a youth ministry consultant in her own right, besides being my wife, gave invaluable help not only on the manuscript, but in formulating these theories in a real partnership over the years. Colleague and friend Jack R. Hoffman offered supportive and thoughtful critique to the early manuscripts as well as being a constant source of encouragement. Debra McEllroy offered helpful suggestions as a youth advisor. The awful chore of typing and retyping went to Barb Smith and Millie Dubs, who labored faithfully and supportively. Finally, there are all the youth advisors and youth themselves whose ministry has touched me beyond their understanding and who are part of each page of this book.

Chapter One
"Well, What Do You Want to Do?" —The Wrong Question

The youth of Trinity Church have been invited to a get-acquainted party in the basement of the church on Sunday night. All of the youth received not only letters addressed to them, but also phone calls about this special party. It has been two years since the Brandts resigned as youth advisors, and this is the first event planned specifically for youth since their resignation.

There has been much discussion since the last organized youth program at Trinity. Certain members of the church board have been concerned that "we'll lose the youth if we don't do something for them." Some of the parents of junior-high-age youth were beginning to wonder if the church cared about their children. "We have to do something to keep the kids off the streets." Even a few of the teens themselves were asking questions. "Why don't we have a youth group here like the one over at Grace Church?"

It was out of this atmosphere and from this history that the party was planned. Pastor Wilson was supportive and encouraging when Mary and Bill Rizzo came to him with the idea. The Rizzos had a daughter, Wendy, who had just gone into seventh grade. Pastor Wilson himself would have done something to try to get the group restarted, but the demands of the parish had kept him too busy. He also believed it was better if the initiative came from those who were concerned, i.e., the parents and youth themselves. Now that the party was planned, he had something positive to report to the board—something was being done.

Fifteen youth showed up for the party. The Rizzos were pleased. Thirty letters had been sent, and as many phone calls had been made. Fifty percent response seemed like a good start.

The party was well planned. There were games to get everyone warmed up. The church basement was redecorated with crepe paper and balloons. A big Welcome sign hung on the back wall. Food had been donated by several parents who also had come along to help with the party. It was an enjoyable evening for everyone.

Near the end of the party, Bill Rizzo announced that he hoped this was the beginning of a new youth group for Trinity Church. He shared the encouragement of Pastor Wilson and the support of the board. Everyone was invited next Sunday night to come to the first organizational meeting of the new youth group.

Bill and Mary were a little disappointed when only ten youth arrived that next Sunday. But they were confident that they could start with that kind of nucleus. After all, excitement had been high during the party.

Mary began the meeting with devotions; then Bill took over at the chalkboard. With chalk in hand, he turned to the assembled group and asked them, "Well, what do you want to do?"

The youth group at Trinity Church began to die at that moment.

The Wrong Question First

Why did the youth group begin to die? What was wrong with Bill's question?

Nothing. There was nothing wrong with the question itself, except that it was asked at the wrong time.

Far too many youth groups begin by asking the wrong question first: What do you want to do? It is a natural mistake. First of all, we live in a do-oriented world. Everything is measured on some kind of scale of achievement or activity.

One way to measure a youth ministry is by its "doings." Obviously, for a youth group to be started, someone must ask the participants what it is they want to do. This was Bill's reasoning in approaching the youth of Trinity Church.

The second reason this question is usually asked first has to do with a philosophy of youth ministry that reasons something like this: "Since the youth group is really for the youth, we need to know what *they* want to do. After all, it's their group." Again, logical reasoning is at work. Bill really did have the youth in mind when he asked his question. It was to be *their* group—so what did they want to do?

Why Is This the Wrong First Question?

With all due respect to logical reasoning and Bill Rizzo's good intentions, this was still the wrong question to ask first. There are four reasons that this is so. First, it is a question that youth very often cannot answer. Ask that question sometime in a group and watch the response. Everyone will start looking around and then staring at the floor. It is difficult to answer because youth are not sure what is possible. No one told them the ground rules. There was no guidance given about what would be acceptable and not acceptable in terms of behavior or ideas or events. They may, indeed, have some ideas, but the teen years are awkward years. Few teens who are struggling for self-acceptance and, at the same time, group acceptance are going to risk saying the wrong thing or making an inappropriate suggestion or laying themselves on the line with an idea until they have some notion about what is possible and acceptable by the group.

Another reason youth have difficulty answering this question is that they often do not really know what they want. This confusion is heightened when there is a new group being formed and none of those present were members of other youth groups. What is a youth group? What is my role in it? What are some things we can do? What will the advisors allow? What will the church allow? What are

21

the expectations? These crucial questions must be dealt with openly and honestly before anyone will risk an idea about *what* to do. If the youth have no history to rely on, no traditions to pick up on, no past experiences to give them ideas for what is possible for them to do, the question is one they cannot answer.

Second, the question "What do you want to do?" is the wrong one to ask because it deals with *wants*. Wants are not only difficult to know and, perhaps for teens, scary to express, they are also the wrong basis for youth ministry programming. For those in positions of leadership in youth ministry, it is important to make the distinction between *wants* and *needs*. A youth program built on wants is always hard to achieve because wants are hard to assess. Wants, by definition, are those things we desire or wish. In youth ministry, it is hard to know what those things are until some groundwork has been laid to discover what is acceptable or proper for a group. For example, many youth enjoy dancing, but can they have a dance in the church? At the first meeting of a new group, no one is going to risk suggesting holding one unless they know something about how the adult advisors feel about it, how the church board will react, and what are the policies on the use of the building.

In starting a youth ministry with wants, the door is open for frustration to set in. The question of wants taps only program knowledge: What was done before? What is possible to do? If a group is new in forming, there is no history, no past experience, to draw on. There is silence and frustration. A youth says in his or her own head: How can I know what I want to do when I don't know what I'm allowed to do? If the group has been together before, programming on wants leads to past orientation. What will be suggested will be what has been done in the past and everyone knows is acceptable. This approach also tends to ignore new members who might have ideas and who certainly have needs, but the pattern is to repeat the past. Next year these new members, if they are still around, can suggest having another hayride.

A better approach to programming is to begin with *needs*. This will be discussed in more detail in chapters 3 and 5. For now, it is enough to be aware that needs are essential for developing a solid youth ministry. Needs—in contrast with wants—imply that something more urgent or essential is lacking. The youth may want to hold a dance, but what they may need is a place to get together to meet other youth, share in some fun, and work off energy. A dance is only one way to meet that need. By programming on needs, a group seeks to meet those needs in creative ways and thus satisfies its members. When youth can be helped to identify those needs and a program is developed to meet them, then the youth ministry of any church will continue to attract and hold the interests of youth. When needs are met, people are satisfied. The old selling motto holds true: a satisfied customer comes back.

Needs build on the present and move toward the future. What was done in the past will be valid only if that particular event meets a present need. Perhaps a dance is not what is needed to bring in new members. Maybe a publicity campaign, personal letters sent to prospective members, phone calls made, or a kidnapping party where the present members legally kidnap new members from their homes and bring them to a youth group meeting might work better. Programming from identified needs leads to a more creative and rewarding approach to youth ministry. The question, What do you want to do? ignores needs. As noted, there will be more on youth needs in subsequent chapters.

The third reason this is the wrong question to ask first is that it is too easy an approach. It is a way to try to develop a youth program quickly and easily. This is certainly an understandable method. In a world of instant needs, fingertip entertainment, and pushbutton conveniences, why not a youth ministry that is quick and easy? Find out what the youth want, help them get it—and an instant youth group is formed.

Unfortunately—or fortunately, depending upon how one examines it—this method of developing a youth program ignores *process*. *How* a youth ministry is developed is as important as the fact that one is formed. Take note of the verbs that have been used so far in this first chapter—create, develop, form. These are all actions that require preparation, planning, and process. A person does not create a great meal by simply reheating whatever can be found in the refrigerator. There is planning involved. A nutritious meal begins with knowing something about balanced diet. Then there is food purchase, preparation (which often takes hours), the actual cooking or baking itself, and, finally, the presentation of an appetizing dish to hungry mouths. There is a process here that cannot be ignored if a person wants to create a balanced, healthy meal. Granted, there are frozen dishes and instant meals, but even they have to be purchased, planned, prepared, and presented.

Youth ministry is no different. There is no such thing as instant, quick-and-easy, heat-and-serve youth ministry. It takes time and effort to develop an effective program that meets the needs of the youth. The way that program gets put together is through a deliberate, intentional process of development. A planning process will be described more fully in chapter 5.

Finally, the What-do-you-want-to-do? question is very often a disguise for some deep-rooted attitudes of those who ask it. It may reflect the "do something" approach. "The youth are there in the church, and someone ought to do something with them." Those who use this approach are concerned because nothing is being done, so the solution is easy. Draw the youth together, find out what they want, and "do" it. This satisfies those who need to see something happening. Unfortunately, no one bothers to find out whether what is being done is what needs to be done or should be done. It becomes youth ministry for the sake of having something labeled "youth ministry."

The "want" approach may often be a disguise for meeting what adults or parents see to be the needs of youth, or even worse, what are really the needs of the adults. For example, parents who are concerned about the influences on their children are clamoring for the church to offer a program which will have a positive influence on them. Pressure is applied to the pastor to do something. He gets a young couple to agree to be youth advisors and start a group.

The parents' attitude here is legitimate. They are truly concerned with the future of their children. They see the church as a possible positive influence and guiding factor for the youth of the community. They begin to raise guilt-producing questions like: Why don't we have a youth program like Grace Church? or, Doesn't our church care about its future? The person who gets hit the hardest by those questions is the pastor. Indeed, he shares the concern for the youth of the community and for the future of the church. However, he has neither the time nor the skill to do youth ministry. A third party now gets involved, usually a young couple, and all the expectations of parents, pastor, and church are suddenly on their shoulders. They are told, "do something" with the youth of Trinity Church.

All these expressed needs are legitimate in their own right. However, the program is started, first of all, to meet the parents' concerns and the pastor's need to meet those concerns. This ignores the situation of the youth themselves. Second, with all those expectations, something had better happen fast; and this leads to the what-do-you-want-to-do? approach. A building, creating, developing process is ignored in the face of adult needs and concerns.

"Well, what do you want to do?" is, indeed, the wrong

25

question to ask first: (1) It is a question that is hard, if not impossible, for youth to answer; (2) it deals with wants first and not needs, which are infinitely more important and basic; (3) it takes a too easy approach to programming and ignores a creative process that can foster growth and development of the group; and (4) it very often belies an underlying intention to meet the needs of adults, namely parents.

Variations on the What-Do-You-Want-to-Do? Theme

Think for a moment about a symphony you like. Remember how the main theme occurs throughout the entire work? Sometimes it is taken up by various instruments or played in different ranges, tempos, or keys. These variations all relate to the central theme of the symphony.

There are also variations on the what-do-you-want-to-do? theme in youth ministry. Some of them are more subtle than others; some are rather obvious.

"What do you kids want?" (How's that for an obvious variation?) Here again, there is implied an adult standing before a group of youth and throwing out a question that lands like a bomb and generally lies there like a dud.

A similar variation goes like this: "Now that we (adults) have called this meeting and gotten you (kids) started, what do you (kids) want to do?" The scene is the same as described in the paragraph above. However, there is some pressure applied from the adults. They called the meeting. They got it started. Now it's time for the kids to do something. "Only an ungrateful kid would not want to respond to our preparation and to our question"—that is the kind of thinking behind what is said. The youth, however, see behind the question and may become frustrated by what they perceive to be subtle manipulation. The adults become frustrated if the youth fail to respond enthusiastically to their initiative.

Or how about this one: "The pastor thinks we ought to do something with the junior-high kids. Let's get them together for a party, have some games and refreshments, and then see what they want to do?" Whose needs are being met? The pressure for starting the group is coming from the pastor. Apparently, he feels the need to "do something," but do the youth feel that same need?

Then there is this variation: "The third week in January is youth week, and time for our youth to do another one of their worship services." In this one, a tradition is used as a means of asking "What do you want to do?" Again, this ties the programming to past experiences and practices without examining whether those practices are relevant for the youth involved in the present.

Youth Ministry for the Wrong Reasons or "We've Got to Do Something with These Kids!"

Without intending to be highly judgmental, and not wanting to belabor this whole issue of the wrong question asked first, I do want to point out there are some very understandable reasons that youth ministry is often approached in this fashion. They are understandable reasons, but they are the wrong reasons to use as a foundation stone in creating or maintaining a youth ministry program.

1) *Fear.* There seems to be an inordinate amount of fear surrounding adults' attitudes and feelings with regard to youth. For parents, it is the fear that their children "won't turn out right." With the influence of drugs, the indications of increasing teen-age drinking, the changing moral scene regarding sex, the impact of violence on T.V., there is bound to be concern for loved ones growing up in these turbulent years of searching.

For the parents of youth who have not yet reached their teens, there is the fear that "if someone doesn't do something now, what's it going to be like when Johnny's in high school." It is a fear of future possibilities. For parents who managed somehow to survive their children's teen

27

years, there is fear for future years with regard to grandchildren.

Our society in general is fearful of where we are going as a country. The churches of our land feel responsible to do something to alleviate some of that fear, to develop a program that "keeps kids off the streets."

2) *Guilt.* Youth ministry is probably one of the strongest guilt producers in any church. Ask any congregation where there is no identifiably active youth group what that church's most glaring needs are, and somewhere near the top of the list there will be "youth ministry." The reasons for this range anywhere from the idea that the youth are the future of the church to the fact that other churches seem to have good programs, "so why can't ours?" This last argument is compounded when the youth of one church attend a going youth group in another church. There is also guilt associated with the history of the church, particularly if there had been an active youth ministry under another pastor.

Add to this internal pressure, the pressure produced by official church agencies, be they regional or national offices, who send out tons of literature describing what Thus-and-so has done, in an effort to encourage other churches to be "that" creative, and the guilt trip is felt pretty strongly. These church-wide agencies are not trying to produce guilt, but the church that has no youth program, or a poorly developed one, perceives this as outside pressure. Combine that pressure with what everyone in the church itself is saying, and guilt can become the motivating factor.

3) *Adult needs.* This reason for starting a youth ministry is an extension of the first two. If a youth group is formed to alleviate the fear or guilt of adults, the motivation meets adult needs, not the needs of the youth. In fact, rarely do people concerned about relieving their own fear and guilt worry about others' needs. It is a "do something" concern that starts from adult perspectives and needs.

28

Intentionality vs. "It's-Sunday-Night-and-Youth-Night-Again"

It is time for a more positive approach. All the reasons just elucidated are reasonable, understandable, and rational. They all deal with doing *something*. However, that does not make them good foundations upon which to start, build, or rebuild a youth ministry program. These reasons can all lead to an "It's-Sunday-night-and-youth-night-again" approach. The basis for doing youth ministry is not laid in a healthy, productive way. There is little positive theory behind just doing *something*.

Those who are involved in youth ministry need a more positive rationale. There needs to be *intentionality*. Intentionality calls for doing the right thing for the right reasons. In youth ministry, this means developing a structure and program that grow out of a clear understanding of what ministry is all about in general, and what youth are all about (i.e., their needs) in particular.

This book is an attempt to provide that kind of positive theory. It is an attempt to provide a theoretical basis for thinking through all parts of a solid youth ministry. The concern here is with more than "What do we do?" It goes beyond that to ask more immediate, pertinent questions, like "Why do we do what we do?" Indeed, "Why youth ministry?"

I hope this book will provide practical, usable advice whether a church is just starting a youth group or has been working at it for some time. There are some admitted biases here. First, and clearly the most important, is that youth ministry does not just happen. It must be worked at, developed, created; and that happens best when there is a sound theological, philosophical, theoretical framework. The second bias is that youth ministry is worth the effort. Otherwise, there would be no need for theory or application.

The book will also deal subsequently with the how-tos of youth ministry. The questions of structure, programs, and advisors will be addressed out of the biases just mentioned. There are no easy answers offered, just some well thought out, practiced observations.

If you are interested in building an effective youth ministry and are willing to accept the biases of hard work and of the importance of that work, read on. Reflect on this material, mull it over, disregard what does not apply, and then create.

Chapter Two

"Where Two or Three Are Gathered Together . . ."
—A Theological Framework

"All you need to do youth ministry these days is a pair of jeans and a good back for sitting on floors," stated Jim Phillips during a break at the annual pastors' conference.

"A beard and guitar wouldn't hurt either," mused Fred Stanley.

"Will you guys please get serious?" Jeff Wagner pleaded. "This is a serious problem. There are too many churches that approach their ministry to youth with that kind of shallowness."

"What are you saying, Fred?" asked Jim.

"I'm saying there should be more to youth ministry than sitting around on the floor and singing songs," Jeff responded. "How a church views its youth is important to the kind of program they will have."

"You know, you're right," Fred reflected. "I never thought of it that way before. In our church, the prevailing attitude is one of 'kids should be seen and heard only once a year at their annual youth service.' "

"And what does that say about our theology?" Jeff responded. "Our attitudes and our practices are outward expressions of what we believe."

"Are you saying we should let the kids do what they want?" asked Fred.

"No, not at all," answered Jeff. "But it's time we stopped playing around in youth ministry and gave it serious thought as an expression of our church and its theology. All of us need to examine our reasons for doing youth ministry in light of the Gospel."

Why youth ministry? That is the question toward which Jim, Fred, and Jeff were working. It is a crucial question and one that requires serious reflection. It is really a theological question. Where is youth ministry grounded?

When building a house, a person does not begin on the second floor and work down. Nor is the place to begin with the plumbing, the electricity, or the furniture. The place to build is on the ground—literally, on the ground. One does not even start with the basement, one starts with the earth, the substance, the piece of dirt from which a house goes upward. There are no windows until there is ground purchased, surveyed, studied, dug into, and that foundation is laid.

Youth ministry also begins on the ground.

"In the Beginning . . ." (Genesis)

There is where it all began—the story of creation. Out of nothing, out of chaos, order was created and took many forms. Placed in charge of this order and bearing responsibility in it were humans. "So God created human beings, making them like himself. . . . God looked at everything he had made, and he was very pleased" (Genesis 1:27, 31 TEV).

From the creation story, two lessons are learned that are relevant to the foundation: (1) The creation of humans in the image of God was not an act of generation-creation. "Humans" implies mankind—all of us who carry the image of God regardless of age, sex, color, or parental origin. Therefore, youth are people, part of God's creation. They get their identity not as youth (a generation identification) but as part of the Creator's design in his image. (2) The creation was pleasing to the Creator. As part of the human race, youth share in the blessing received by that creation. There is no intended favoritism of generations, sexes, or races. Youth are part of the design, a blessed part, a pleasing part, but only a part.

Perhaps this is stating the obvious, but there are too many

churches that go to extremes in their youth ministry and base those extremes on a thoughtless theology that ignores creation. There are churches that seek to make of youth ministry a separate entity within its fellowship, as if youth are a breed apart. They are relegated to youth rooms, told not to dirty other parts of the building, and asked only to come out and perform at the once-a-year youth service.

There is also the other extreme—the church that caters to its youth with a specialness not given other groups. Everything possible is done *for* them, while other parts of God's good creation get little, if any, attention. The problem with this approach is that it overemphasizes one area of ministry and often ignores other important and needed concerns. The young adults and their needs, for instance, should not be ignored because all the time and energy of the church is being channeled to the youth.

The story of creation remains incomplete, and there is a serious distortion in our view of human nature unless Genesis 3 is considered. Human beings were not content to live obediently and peacefully in the middle of God's good creation. There was rebellion; there is sin, and youth are as much a part of that world as they are a part of the creation story. As Adam and Eve were not content, wanting what they could not have, and ultimately turning away from their Creator in willful disobedience, so all who share humanity share in the freedom of willful choices that often lead away from God. Youth are part of this whole creation story— created good by a loving Creator, given free will, not perfect in their choices, and by nature sinful. Church youth are no different from others in sharing this common story.

The Example of Jesus

There is a saying going around Christian education circles that has some relevance to this issue. The saying goes like this: "In Christian education we do just the opposite of what Jesus did. He taught the adults and played with the kids; we play with the adults and teach the kids." There is much wisdom in that saying.

In youth ministry, it is important to raise the same kind of question. Do we follow the example of Jesus? How did he treat young people, those somewhere between childhood and adulthood?

The answers are not that simple. Jesus did say, "Let the children come to me, and hinder them not" (Luke 18:16). However, the way to approach this issue is not so much through what Jesus said, as through what he did. The only written record of Jesus as a growing youth is an indication of something of his spirit. At the age of twelve, Jesus accompanied his parents to Jerusalem for the feast of the Passover. Jesus left his parents and, of all things, was discovered in the temple talking with the teachers. He listened and asked questions, and people who heard him were amazed at his understanding.

Before conclusions can be drawn, reflect on another scene in Jesus' life. Eighteen years later, Jesus was back in the temple, according to Matthew, Mark, and Luke. There was a debate raging among his followers as to who was the greatest. Jesus listened for a time; then he took a child (sex unknown) and placed the child in the middle of the gathering. Then he spoke these words: "I assure you that unless you change and become like children, you will never enter the Kingdom of heaven. The greatest in the Kingdom of heaven is the one who humbles himself and becomes like this child. And whoever welcomes in my name one such child as this, welcomes me" (Matthew 18:3-5 TEV).

There are many examples that could be enumerated. It is interesting to note that the vast majority of Jesus' dealings with children are recorded in all three Synoptic Gospels (Matthew, Mark, and Luke). That in itself is not significant, but the way he related to children is. First of all, there was no age bias. Children were part of the Kingdom. They were not to be sent away to an educational wing somewhere while the adults got down to the serious business of discussing the Kingdom. Second, there are no references to age groupings beyond the descriptive "little" used occasionally. Teens were considered part of the adult world—they married, had children, held jobs, were initiated into adulthood in early teen years. Jesus' use of such words as "little," "old," and "children" was always meant to be descriptive, not judgmental or demeaning. Jesus dealt with people as people, part of creation blessed by the Creator. Indeed, his whole mission centered around them—all of them.

When the teachings of Jesus are examined, the same kinds of attitudes can be noted. Take the famous parable of the prodigal son (Luke 15:11-32). Two sons, both treated fairly by their father, each chose separate ways to live. The one stayed at home; the other left to find fun and happiness. When the younger returned home penniless and penitent, the father was there to greet him with open arms even before the confession of wrong could be stated. Here, dramatically displayed, is love and forgiveness.

The question is, was that parable told for adults only (a kind of X-rated story), or was it for all who had ears to hear and eyes to see? The answer is plain. Jesus' teachings were directed to all persons who shared in hearing the Good News. Therefore, all the teachings of Jesus apply to children. What he said about love and forgiveness is a story they need to hear. What he spoke about witnessing and discipleship are lessons they need to learn. What he shared about the Kingdom includes those with little hands and ears.

Paul Johnson wrote in the January 1979 issue of *Learning With:* "The place of children in the church corresponds with the place of children in the thinking of Jesus. We cannot improve upon it, we can only implement it."[1] From the example of both the teachings and dealings with children by Jesus, it is clear that he included them totally and without reservation. They are part of the creation, part of humankind, part of the Good News he came to bring.

The Community of Faith

"Our youth are the future of the church," exclaimed Jed Phillips, long-time member of First Church. "We need to have a good youth program because our youth today are the leaders of the church in the future."

"I agree," chimed in Sally Miller. "Those kids are the future church. We need to guide and develop their leadership, or the church is in big trouble."

Fred Jacobs could stand it no more; finally he felt compelled to ask, "Are the kids tomorrow's church, or are they today's church?"

This dialogue is a very clear example of how many people in churches feel about the youth—"They are tomorrow's church." That is true, as far as it goes. However, as Fred Jacobs rightfully pointed out, that view ignores the place of youth in today's church. It is true that the future leaders of the church, of business, of society in general are the youth of today. But is that all youth are in the church, a future? What about the church today?

It is time to reexamine this community of faith called the church and to explore the role of youth in it. What is the church? The church is the people of God who have a *message* to proclaim and a *mission* to fulfill. The message is the Good News (i.e., Gospel) that in Jesus Christ, God acted to save the world. The mission of the church is to go out and proclaim that message of Christ in the world.

A congregation is an identified group of the people of God who share in hearing the message and in fulfilling the mission. In any congregation, regardless of denomination, certain ways of living out its mission are fostered. These can be identified as the functions of a congregation. Among the many that can be listed, there are four basic ones: worship, teach, witness, and serve. The message gets proclaimed and the mission gets fulfilled as each of these are done.

Who does these acts (functions)? The members of the

congregation who have identified themselves either in their baptism or dedication as the people of God do them. These are not the roles of the clergy alone. All the people of God are to be about them. We share in these tasks because we are God's people.

One of the roles of the church, therefore, is to *equip* its members to be God's people, i.e., to be doing and participating in the various functions of the church. If this is all true, then the role of the youth within any church and any specific congregation is to be a part of its mission. Youth are not only the church of tomorrow, they are a vital, active part of the church today. They are partners in mission. They are participants in the functions. Their place is to be part of the ministry of the church. They are recipients and transmitters like everyone else. They receive training, are equipped to be God's agents in the world, and are his instruments as they share in the ministry of his church.

The "church-of-the-future" notion of youth ignores two things: (1) that youth are part of the people of God now, and (2) that youth are contributors to, not only receivers of, the ministry of any church.

Why Youth Ministry?

It is now time to ask the ultimate question, Why youth ministry? This is a perfectly legitimate question and, indeed, one that needs to be wrestled with as the foundation is laid. From the theological discussion on creation, and the examples of Jesus, the church, and its ministry, seven answers can be given. Not all of them will appear as logical deductions, but they do grow out of what has been shared. It is important to keep in mind that youth ministry is part of the total ministry of the church and can never be viewed apart from that ministry.

1) Youth ministry recognizes the uniqueness of the *needs* of youth. Every age group has its own unique flavor. What is important to youth may not be important to adults. What

adults need for their growth and nurture is different from what a young child needs. A youth ministry program recognizes the uniqueness of youth needs and strives to minister to and with the youth.

2) Youth ministry recognizes the unique gifts of youth. As children of God and partners in his mission, youth have something to contribute to the church. A good youth ministry program is developed around the acknowledgment of these gifts and the attempt to draw on this rich, valuable resource in the church.

3) Youth ministry is a part of the life of the church. It is not only a responsibility as the church strives to care for persons at all points in their lives, it is also an opportunity to guide, counsel, and direct persons during an impressionable time in their lives. This is part of the equipping that the church does for its members. The teen years are ripe years for this to be fostered.

4) Youth ministry can develop a wholistic approach to people and to life in general. Youth need to be approached and understood as *total* beings. The church has the opportunity to encourage and foster the growth and development of all aspects of a person. This is especially accomplished in balanced programming (see chapter 5).

5) Youth need a place and a space to interact beyond the school system and athletic field. This interaction crosses over school lines, as a given church may encompass a number of school systems. It also crosses over age and sex boundaries, especially important in early teen years. There is also the healthy interaction that occurs between adults and youth.

6) The church can offer significant models for youth. Beyond mere interaction, the adults involved in youth ministry become living examples of the Christian life. This does not mean that youth leaders need to be saints. It does mean that youth need examples that they can see and relate to. The church can offer those live examples at a time when youth are impressionable (see chapter 6).

7) Youth need to be integrated into the life of the church. It is a truism that people do not feel a part of something unless they participate. Youth ministry offers that involvement at an acceptable level. It is a training area for future leaders, but it is also an arena for involvement in the mission of the church now. This is not a case for doing away with a separate, structured youth program. Some recent studies indicate that youth are more effectively integrated into the life of the church when a structured youth program is fostered. The youth group offers an arena for mission and leadership to occur, an arena that youth are comfortable in. As a balanced program is fostered, youth participate in all the functions of the church and become integrated through experience and exposure.

Why youth ministry? For these reasons and a host more. These are positive foundations upon which to build. By understanding something of the church, its functions, and the role of youth in the church, a solid, sound youth program can be created. What do you want to do?—the question of chapter 1—can soon be asked because there is an understanding of what it is that *should* be done.

The ground has been prepared in this chapter. Now it's time to build the basement of the house. Chapter 3 goes beyond the theological framework to deal with an understanding of who youth are. We need to further explore youth needs and uniquenesses as we create this house called youth ministry.

Chapter Three
"Kids Are Kids"
—And Other Myths

"When I was a kid they didn't have programs for us," Jim Sealy shouted. "We weren't catered to like these kids today are. We had to work as soon as we were old enough."

"That's true," responded Mary James. "We didn't expect people to do things for us. We did 'em ourselves."

"But that was back then," added Frank Wilson. "Things are different now."

Are things different now? Can a conclusion be drawn that "a kid is a kid is a kid" regardless of the day and age in which he or she lives?

Where Are the Youth of Today?

Take this test. Read the following statements and then determine if they are generally true or generally false as applied to youth. Think of the youth you know.

1) Youth are not interested in mass protest or students' rights.
2) They appear to be future-oriented and practical.
3) They have little concern for development of creativity or appreciation for the arts and humanities.
4) Reading outside of the school classroom is limited.
5) They believe the greatest global problems to be overpopulation and the environment.
6) Abortion is an issue which divides youth.
7) About one-half of all youth say they cannot comfortably talk with their parents about personal problems.
8) The great majority believe drugs to be the single worst influence on youth today.

9) The majority do not see themselves as affected by pornography or the relaxation of sexual standards.
10) The women's liberation movement has had little impact upon girls of high-school age.
11) Less than one-fourth rank religion as an issue of major importance as they view their lives in the next five years.
12) Financial expectations are of considerable concern.
13) The great majority state they will forsake fame and fortune for happiness.

Believe it or not, all these statements are true. They represent a sample of findings in a survey taken by the National Association of Secondary School Principals.[1] The point of this exercise was to point out how difficult it is to identify these creatures labeled "youth." We tend to base our generalizations on observations. After all, that is the scientific method we were taught. The problem here is that our observations are not broad enough—we see and note only that which is within our vision—nor are they consistent enough to allow data generalization. When dealing with human behavior, personal observations which lead to generalizations can be misleading. Not all youth hang out on street corners, but some do. To make a general statement that all youth are lazy, based on the youth seen standing idly on corners, is to go one step beyond fairness. Not all teens spend their days leaning against light posts. Not even the majority of teens are found there.

Therefore, generalizations about who youth are, what they think and feel, and where they are going can be dangerous. National surveys like the one noted earlier are helpful in giving a broader perspective. Frank Wilson was right. "Things are different these days." As the song goes, "The times, they are a changin'!" Recognizing some of those changes and the biases people have concerning them will help those who work with youth to be more open and accepting in relating to young people today.

Who Are the Youth of Today?

Surveys are helpful in attempting to discover who youth are and what they think. *Life* magazine ran a special fall issue in 1977 called The New Youth. Although their study included a broader age spectrum (ages fifteen to the mid-twenties) than this book is dealing with, their findings have some validity for those who work with youth. Again being careful about what is done with overgeneralizations, the *Life* report indicated that youth are "bright, worrisome, suspicious of promises (especially from elders). . . . They appear to have a firm rein on their own enthusiasms and are not quick to commit themselves. They are practical. They are careful with their choices. They are capable of forceful and intelligent comment on their concerns and on what lies ahead for them. . . . At the same time as they are caring of each other, they are not a passionate generation—or perhaps more correctly, their passions are less visible and audible than those say, of the youth ten years ago."

It is true that "kids are kids are kids," but that oversimplification is not helpful. While wanting to relate to teens in constructive, nonjudgmental ways, the kids-are-kids-are-kids approach neglects two important things: (1) youth are people, and, as people, are all different and unique (recall chapter 2); and (2) there are factors that affect all people in a society of rapid change. The world is different now than it was ten years ago. Those changes must be noted in order not to make inappropriate judgments about values and attitudes today. The example at the beginning of the chapter is a case in point. Jim Sealey made a judgment on youth today based on his experience years ago—a dangerous and demeaning thing to do.

It is possible, however, to note *trends,* and these can be very significant for those who minister with youth. Although there have been numerous surveys done, one of the most helpful for persons in youth ministry was the 1978 Youth Concerns Survey[2] conducted through the Division for Parish

Services of the Lutheran Church in America. This survey has validity because it was broad in participation—youth from twelve states and provinces in the United States and Canada. Participants included junior- and senior-high youth, Lutheran and non-Lutheran, active and inactive church members. The following statements outline some trends based on the survey results which are pertinent to understanding who youth are today.

1) Each youth is unique with different interests and concerns. There is little agreement among youth about specific concerns.

2) Youth want and need to be seen as persons. They are concerned about establishing their identity. Relationships with peers, concern for personal appearance, and relationships with adults support this need.

3) Relationships are a major concern for youth. They are concerned about relating with parents, brothers and sisters, peers and adults.

4) The larger and more distant the issues are from youth, the less concern they have. National and world issues and concern for the future rank low among youth except as they touch their personal lives.

5) Attitudes toward school seem to be primarily those of meeting the requirements to get out. Key issues include grades, tests, and studying.

6) Youth are looking toward the future, concerned primarily about marriage and jobs.

7) Moral issues focus on three areas: sex, drugs, and drinking. Youth who are not active in church tend to express greater concern about moral issues than youth who are active in church.

8) Theological questions rank high among youth. Active youth ask, "What is God like?" while those not active in church ask the more basic question, "Does God exist?" The inactive youth are asking the basic questions about the reality of God, which need to be answered before

the next question about the nature of God can be approached.

9) Youth tend to have a concern about their doubts.

10) Although the youth in the survey say they are "satisfied" with the church, other responses point toward a general dissatisfaction. All youth say, "It isn't planned for youth." Inactive youth are generally turned off and say the church "isn't relevant." All youth suggest that the church ought to be involved in social issues.

Who are the youth today? The surveys are helpful in painting a broader picture than personal observations tend to do. The answer is easy, but not simple. Youth are people, and people are not simple creatures to understand, much less explain. The broad trends outlined in the surveys noted are helpful as long as quick judgments and simple generalizations are avoided.

Are Church Youth Different?

If the approach that says kids-are-kids-are-kids can be done away with, there is another myth that needs to be destroyed. Many people assume that youth who are actively involved in churches and their own youth groups are different. These are "the future leaders of society, groomed in our churches." Unfortunately, facts and statistics do not support this myth. It is equally impossible to apply any one label to all church youth as it is to all youth universally.

Dr. Merton P. Strommen, research psychologist, clergyman, and head of the Youth Research Center in Minneapolis, conducted an excellent study of over seven thousand young people across the country and including the entire denominational spectrum. The results of his study are found in the book *Five Cries of Youth*.[3] In answer to the question, Are church youth different? Strommen discovered some interesting data. He found that church and nonchurch youth are alike in their reactions to common adolescent problems.

These common problems are identified as parental understanding, dating, lack of self-confidence, academic problems, and classroom relationships. He also discovered similarities in the political/social attitudes of church and nonchurch youth.

However, his study did reveal some interesting differences. First of all, there were marked differences in beliefs and values. Church youth tend to be more people-oriented and for that reason differed from nonchurch youth in the following areas: sense of moral responsibility; desire for a meaningful life; religious participation; social action; self-regard; feeling for people; and God awareness. Second, with contrasts in beliefs and values, there were also noted some contrasts in life-style. This was demonstrated basically in lower incidence of premarital sex, drinking, and drug use among youth of the church as compared with those of the nonchurch group.

What does all this mean? Are youth today radically different from young people ten, fifteen, or twenty years ago? If a person tries to answer that question by examining fads and moods, the answer is yes, but looking beneath the cultural surface produces a different answer. Modern psychological studies and extensive sociological surveys have indicated that the values, beliefs, attitudes, and concerns of youth are remarkably consistent, irrespective of time, culture, and location. Those who work with youth should be aware of the uniqueness of those we label "teen."

Characteristics of the Adolescent Years

Developmental psychologists have been able to identify the characteristics or marks of various age groups. These are the issues, or the developmental tasks, that are peculiar to a particular time of life. The often turbulent teen years are no different. There are five basic issues that are special in any individual young person's life. These are identified simply as the five I's of youth.

45

1) *Identity.* During the adolescent years, a person makes the transition from a childhood image to an image of himself or herself as an adult. One of the chief marks of maturity is the ability to set goals, release creative energy, relate effectively with others, have a sense of personal worth, meaning, purpose, and peace in life. It could be called "discovering one's calling." This search for self-identity consumes a large measure of time and energy during the teen years.

2) *Independence.* Another mark of growing maturity is the ability to take responsibility for one's actions. Sometimes it is called "owning up." It is the difference between reacting to things that happen and making things happen. It is also demonstrated in the difference between blaming other people and taking control of one's own life. Philosophically, it means not being blown and controlled by the winds of chance, but rather taking a stance against the givens and inevitables of life. It means wanting to make a creative, personal contribution to the world. During these teen years a person makes the transition from dependency to interdependency. These are tough years for parents, as teens need to experiment and gain strength on their own. Much rebelliousness has its roots in this struggle.

3) *Intimacy.* The ability to relate to others as persons rather than as objects for one's own use is another sign of growth toward maturity. Sometimes it is called "loving our enemies." The marks of this developmental struggle are obvious in teens. The sorting out of one's own feelings of maleness and femaleness, the ability to relate to others as sexual beings, the ability to confirm the other's freedom, even the fight to overcome oppression and to work for justice in the world are but a few of the tasks involved. It is during these teen-age years that the transition from possessing others to loving them is made. The meaning of human relationships is explored during this time, and the church can be crucial to that exploration and in that struggle.

4) *Inspiration.* These years are literally the time of grand and glorious dreams. It is the time when the transition takes place from preoccupation with one's own bodily and psychological needs to an idealistic vision of what life and the world could be. Adults often refer to it as "the idealism of youth" or "looking at the world with rose-colored glasses." This ability to look at the world with a fresh perspective can be and often is a powerful force in bringing about needed changes. On the other hand, "practical" adults can stifle this creative visioning and energy by not listening to or putting down those who dream big dreams.

5) *Investment.* During these transition years, a person begins to make the change from letting others care about persons and causes to developing significant commitments of one's own. The commitment to some cause or causes in life is still another indication of developing maturity. It could be called "laying down your life for your friends." It has to do with deep caring. It means identifying the primary meanings and values of life. One takes ultimate ownership for oneself.

An argument could be made for the fact that these characteristics are really the aims of all people no matter what their age. That is true to a large extent. However, the struggle for maturity begins to take place during the teen-age years. These developmental tasks can be acute and even painful. A church interested in youth, and more particularly, a group of adults who work with them need to be reminded of some of these struggles. Awareness can lead to greater understanding. If youth ministry can be labeled as any one thing, it is *relationships;* and those relationships develop around mutual understanding.

Five Cries of Youth

The study by Merton P. Strommen has already been mentioned in this chapter. This work is probably the most significant survey taken of youth in recent years. It has particular value for those persons who work in youth ministry, because not only does Dr. Strommen identify five areas of need or value orientation (which he labels "cries"), he suggests from his findings some ways that the church can more effectively minister to the youth of today. Any youth ministry that strives to be intentional in its approach needs to be aware of the areas of need and points of struggle for the youth that share in that ministry.

Strommen's evidence led him to the conclusion that any relational gap between youth and their parents is really the same gap which older adults knew as young people. The way this gap gets expressed is indeed different. The outward life-styles have varied over the years. Fads and moods have changed. But if the substance underneath these changes is examined, there is no change. These five cries are universal and timeless expressions of needs or values. Like the characteristics of adolescent years, these are the ways in which all youth are alike.

Defining the five cries of youth is simply another way to identify the internal issues that all youth face. As before, identifying the struggle can lead to greater understanding. A youth ministry built on an understanding of the value struggles and need issues of youth is developing on a solid foundation. The five cries identified by Stommen are summarized briefly below, along with some of the implications for youth ministry in particular.

1) *Self-Hatred.* Expressed in feelings of worthlessness, self-criticism, and loneliness, this cry of self-hatred is the most intense and frequent of the cries of youth. Among youth who expressed this cry, eight factors were frequently found—three dealing with feelings about self, and five dealing with feelings about others:

　a) feelings of personal failure
　b) a lack of self-confidence
　c) loneliness resulting from a low estimate of self-worth
　d) bothersome classroom relationships

  e) academic problems
  f) concern over family relationships
  g) anxiety over one's relationship to God
  h) concern about relationships with the opposite sex—
     particularly concern over finding a life partner.

Youth expressing this cry are often helped through loving relationships. Help can come through friends, teachers, parents, and through affirmation and genuine adult interest. As stated earlier, youth ministry needs to be developed on a sound theological framework. Here is the place where that theology becomes real. Youth ministry is not intended to be a therapy group for troubled teens. The focus should not be on problem-solving, i.e., overcoming youth's fears, gaining confidence, improving self-esteem. Those are the by-products, the positive results, of a youth ministry that develops wholesome, caring relationships between persons. Youth need to know they are loved (who loved us first?), are important, have potential, and can look forward to positive change. It is through the living example of people who embody God's message of love and acceptance (those who live and practice the mission of the church) that a youth's awareness can be changed. True, personal concern and outward warmth are the key factors. The important implication for youth ministry in this first cry of youth is not to learn problem-solving techniques or to have degrees in psychology. An empathic and warm relationship with a concerned person makes the difference. Since warmth and concern are the qualities needed, then untrained people and indeed both youth and adults can minister to one another.

  2) *Psychological Orphans.* This cry is an expression of the need of a young person to be part of a family whose members love and accept and care about one another. Many youth are preoccupied with distressing family situations, often caused by the following four factors:

  a) family pressures—often a troubled relationship with
     one of the parents;

49

    b) distress over parental relationships—lack of under-
       standing, poor communication, parents distrustful or
       too strict;
    c) a lack of closeness in family—especially when parents
       don't get along;
    d) a lack of social concern—family is unresponsive to
       needs outside the home.

This cry arises from youth who desperately need the stability, support, and love of a home that they do not have to earn or deserve.

The church can be extremely helpful. Influencing and changing parental attitudes is an appropriate goal for a church. As parents are helped to love each other, to establish a climate of trust, and to begin honest, open communication with their teen-age children, positive changes will be seen.

A youth ministry can serve as a loving support group for youth who need care and support because it is not available at home. A fellowship, in the best sense of that word, can provide a depth of relationship, a security, an honesty of communication with which a youth can identify. Again, the focus is not on being a therapy group, but on being a group of caring people who live out the gospel of love and forgiveness and who share in the fruits of the Holy Spirit (love, joy, peace, patience, kindness, gentleness, self-control). A youth program developed on that kind of foundation grows.

3) *Social Protest (Outrage).* The third cry of youth is perhaps the most subtle. Socially concerned youth display five general characteristics:

    a) humanitarian concern—especially for suffering peo-
       ple—combined with consciousness and clarity of their
       values and beliefs;
    b) a desire for change (in specific areas);
    c) involvement in helping activities;
    d) concern with national issues;
    e) criticism of the institutional church because they
       perceive adults as not caring.

In response to this cry, the church needs to say clearly, "We care," and to say it in positive action. A creative youth ministry offers opportunities for youth to express and act on their social concerns. It will also provide ways to help youth clarify their beliefs and values. This can turn true social concern and internal feeling of outrage into a positive expression of doing something for another's good. The Gospel can become lived out in positive action in a youth ministry that seeks to serve. Strommen discovered that the factors that made a youth ministry most effective were candor and caring among the members. Four out of five youth would go out of their way to attend meetings where people "felt free to say what they really think" and to experience acceptance among people "who really care about each other." These are solid foundations upon which to build.

4) *Prejudice (Closed Minds).* In describing the cry of the prejudiced, Strommen identified two styles of religion—one motivated by internal commitment, and one which stresses achieving God's favor through one's own efforts. It is the age-old struggle of law versus gospel. The law orientation says a person finds favor with God through his own efforts (living the law). The Gospel orientation states that a person finds favor with God only through God's grace (his unconditional, first love of us). The cry of the prejudiced youth is the cry of a law orientation and is characterized in the following ways:
   a) affirming a religion which stresses achievement and doing one's best;
   b) prejudice toward those not of same race, class, or social standing;
   c) loyalty to the institutional church;
   d) self-oriented values;
   e) concern over national issues.

The church can best minister to these youth through an educational approach which confronts stereotypes, stimulates reflection, and clarifies the truth of God's grace. A youth ministry that strives to be wholistic will need to see itself as an educational arm of the church as well as a social arm. The cry of the prejudiced is one of the hardest to respond to and yet one of the most important. Sound theological principles and a practicing faith based on a Gospel orientation are important.

5) *Joy.* One of the most insistent and frequent of the cries of youth is that of the joyous. Joy which stems from a sense of identity and mission centered in Christ is reflected in values, beliefs, and perceptions. Characteristics of these youth include:

a) identification with a personal, caring God;
b) involvement in a religious community;
c) motivation to grow and develop;
d) social action.

This cry typifies one out of three church youth, according to Strommen. These are youth who identify with a God who loves them and with a people who care about them. It is the cry of a whole person. In a sense, this is what youth ministry should be all about—helping to develop a God-relationship; fostering religious participation; and developing an ethical life characterized by moral responsibility, a caring attitude, and a positive outlook. For these youth, the Christian faith provides a positive, moral force and helps them personally develop a hopeful and positive life perspective.

Who are the youth of today? They are a rich and exciting blend of diversity and uniqueness. The social-psychological perspectives set forth in this chapter are simply models for understanding something of who youth are. Overgeneralizations that lead to biased views are not called for here. Rather, these models are suggested so that an open, aware attitude which grows out of a theology of love and caring can be developed. To continue with our youth ministry house, these are the stones of the foundation. A youth ministry developed on "wants" tries to bypass what takes time and courage to build—a solid foundation based on knowing who we are (i.e., Christ's) and who youth are as they struggle through some difficult developmental years.

Youth Ministry by Preposition

Intentional youth ministry begins with the whys and wherefores. It means creating from a solid foundation. As our theology tells us to live in love and service to others, the beginning point for youth ministry is the youth themselves. Who are they? Where are they? Hence, this chapter is essential.

Now it is time to ask the relational questions that help determine the working philosophy for youth ministry. Examine youth ministry *by preposition* and notice the questions that are raised.

1) Is youth ministry, ministry *for* youth? The obvious answer to this is yes. This entire chapter has dealt with identifying the needs, issues, and characteristics of the persons for whom youth ministry is intended. However, this is not as obvious an answer as it may seem. As pointed out before, much that passes as youth ministry is ministry for adults—ministry that alleviates adult fears, quiets adult guilt, or meets adult needs. The preposition "for" identifies the proper target for the ministry. Knowing who the ministry is for helps determine not only the program but also the style of that ministry. A ministry for senior citizens is different from a ministry for youth. The content may be similar (meet needs, provide opportunities for fellowship, develop relationships) but the style (the way it gets done) will be different.

2) Is youth ministry, ministry *with* youth? Again, a yes. If youth ministry merely stopped at being "for" youth, the direction of that ministry would always be *toward* the youth. Ministry would become something done "for" them or "to" them. But as our theology made clear, youth are part of God's people and part of his church. This puts them into relationship—with one another, with adults who work with

them, and with the whole church. The "with" preposition represents the interrelationships in ministry. Youth and adults, youth and youth, youth in the church, all working together to be God's people, to live the mission, to proclaim the message of the Good News.

3) Is youth ministry, ministry *by* youth? Absolutely! The acknowledgment of the gifts that youth bring to the church is essential in any working philosophy of youth ministry. They are contributing parts of the church of today. They have ministry to give to one another, in the church and in the world. The "by" preposition represents the awareness and encouragement of young people as part of the church of today.

Intentional youth ministry recognizes all three prepositions as essential in a working philosophy. Youth ministry is ministry for, with, and by youth. It is the statement that the clear focus of the ministry is youth; it is a partnership ministry which strives to develop and encourage the youth to live out their own ministries.

The House Is Growing

The house called youth ministry is getting a good start. Theological foundations have been laid. An understanding of youth has been shared. A prepositional philosophy has been proposed. Now, how do we gather the troops together? Or, to keep the analogy straight, how do we build the first floor?

Youth ministry now becomes a matter of structure—literally, structure. How do we organize into some kind of shape or pattern what we know about the church, about youth, about a working philosophy of youth ministry? Read on.

Chapter Four
How Are "Two or Three Gathered Together . . ."?
—The Structural Issue

"The best way to structure a youth program is the way we've always done it," commented Les Myers at the regional youth workers meeting. "We use officers elected by the kids themselves. That way we know who's doing what. Then we advisors just advise."

"Well, our kids need a lot of help in organizing," reflected June Akers. "They don't know how to do good planning, so the adults end up doing it all or it doesn't get done. I guess our way of organizing is to have the adults plan it and hope the kids will participate."

"We try to involve our youth in planning and organizing," added June Fry. "We have a planning committee that is responsible for putting together our program. The advisors and some youth elected by the group form this committee. We've never tried it with officers or advisors doing it all. This approach seems to work for us."

"What is the best way to organize the group?" Jim Baker asked. "We're just trying to get our youth program going, and we want to do it right. What's the best approach?"

A good question: What is the best way to organize? The answer requires a good deal of thought. It is possible that the youth programs represented by Les, June, and June are all structured correctly. It is also possible that each one could stand some restructuring. How can a group tell the difference?

Examine first the purposes for structuring. There are two: (1) structuring helps a group to do (or accomplish) that which

55

it sets out to do, and (2) structuring develops lines of responsibility for that doing to get done. To ask, What is the best way to organize? one must ask, What is it you want to accomplish, and who is going to do it? Therefore, what is best for one group may not be good for another.

Where to Begin?

The answer to that question may be so obvious that it need not be restated. Since it took three chapters to get to the question of organizational structure, the answer is clear: with a solid foundation. There are three parts to this foundation:

1) *Theological Base.* Any church or group of persons intent on developing a youth program needs to ask the question, Why? The answer must be grounded in an understanding of the church and the role of youth in it. This is where identity gets developed. A church youth group should be different from a school social club, or a fraternity, or the youth auxiliary of the Rotary Club, or a sports organization. By thinking through its groundings, a church begins to develop a structure and then a program for its youth ministry from that base.

2) *The Youth.* The structure should also reflect an understanding of the basic characteristics of youth and an awareness of the particularities of the youth to be involved in that program. For example, a small church with few youth may decide to keep one group rather than to divide along junior/senior high grade levels. A church with predominantly younger teens involved will organize differently from one that has mostly older teens. The younger teens may need more supervision and adult involvement in the structure.

3) *Goals.* Based on the needs of those the ministry is intended to serve, what does the group want to accomplish? The basic goals for the organization need to be examined (goals will be discussed more in chapter 5). A group that has as its primary goal to develop youth leadership may need a different type of structure than one which has relationship

building as its primary goal. Organizing to meet stated goals also allows for flexibility and builds them into its thinking from the start. Therefore, as goals change, so will the organizational structure to allow for those goals to be met.

Principles of Structuring

The term "structuring" used throughout this chapter refers to the way the overall group is designed or set up to enable its program to function—in other words, organizing to do what a group *wants to do*. A similar term is "organizational structure." It is the framework (after a solid foundation has been laid) within which the program operates. Six principles of structuring are important as a youth group is organized.

1) *Size*. The overall size of the group needs to be examined. A group of twelve youth may function well without designated leaders with each person taking some responsibility. A group of sixty youth needs a more sophisticated structure. Designated leaders, perhaps officers, need to be appointed or elected.

With regard to size, there are some obvious constraints. The larger the group, the more structure is needed. In fact, the larger the group, the greater the need for identified strong leadership. Someone must assume responsibility. Also, the larger the group, the more time is needed to "oil the machinery." More energy and time must go into maintaining a complex organization than a small, simple one. The secret here is not to develop such a complex structure that all the time and creative energy of the leaders go into maintaining it. It is important to oil any machine to keep it functioning, but the end result is not the machine itself but rather what the machine produces. In youth ministry terms, the end result of structure is a youth program, not the structure itself.

2) *Needs and Goals*. Since the structure of any organization is not an end in itself, the way a group is structured depends

on the identified needs and established goals of that particular group. A group that wants to focus its program on serving the church as its primary goal will organize itself differently from one that sees developing adult/youth relationships as its primary goal. The age of those involved is also a factor in goals and needs. This affects structuring also.

3) *Effectiveness vs. Efficiency.* Too many organizations are structured on the principle of efficiency. Businesses strive for it because efficiency means getting the most out of the least. Profits are determined in large measure by how efficiently an operation runs.

However, the efficiency principle is not the best way to organize a youth program. Organizing around effectiveness is better. In youth ministry, efficiency means producing a definite result. The difference is subtle but important. Structuring for effectiveness means organizing so as to produce a desired outcome. The effort may be as important as the result. Very often, the desired outcome is helping the youth to take greater responsibility, to try new tasks, to grow as people. If organized around efficiency, and a minimum effort is the result, a program or task might be done by a select few time and again because they know how to do it well. There is no place for new people to try; there is no place for growth of the individual, no place to develop new skills.

4) *Accountability.* This is a big word for "Who's responsible?" Since one of the purposes for structure in the first place is to ensure that the program gets done, that "getting done" implies that someone or some persons are going to do it. An organizational structure should clearly indicate lines of responsibility. The buck has to stop somewhere; structure tells an organization where.

Corporations design what are called organizational flow charts to show clearly how the corporation is organized to function. People know who is accountable to whom and so on. Youth groups should be able to design the same kind of chart. Some questions that may help determine that chart are:

Who is answerable to whom? Where does the buck stop? How does communication flow in the organization, and from whom does it start? Developing clear lines of responsibility is important not only so that things get done by the proper persons, but also as a way to develop responsibility and leadership in an organization. This is especially important for youth.

5) *Continuity.* One of the recurrent problems among churches with youth programs has been what is labeled the roller-coaster effect. Very simply, this means that a youth program will develop and slowly increase in size and effectiveness. After the group of youth who have been involved during this growth period leaves for jobs or college, the bottom seems to drop out of the program. Then the building and developing must begin again. This roller-coaster effect normally runs about a three-year cycle. A core group becomes involved, and leadership is determined by it. The group hangs together for three years, rarely changing or sharing leadership and rarely inviting outsiders in. In about three years, when they leave, the church is left to develop a whole new program.

A well-developed structure builds in continuity. It allows for and fosters new and changing leadership, but the structure supports the group through it all. The people in positions of leadership may change, and indeed should change periodically, but the responsibilities within the structure do not. As long as those responsibilities get carried out, the organization will continue to function. New ideas, new programs, new projects can always be initiated because the structure can support them. Continuity is an important organizing principle for youth ministry.

6) *Planners vs. Doers.* There is an obvious difference between planning and doing. There is also a difference in people who are planners and people who are doers. One of the major mistakes in youth ministry is to put doers into planners' roles. The result is a high level of frustration.

59

People who are doers want to use their energies in the doing of an activity. Sitting down and planning an event is not their idea of getting something done.

In structuring a group it is important to identify the doers and the planners. As a structure is organized, fitting the right person into the right role becomes crucial. This does not mean pigeonholing people or not challenging them to grow in new areas. It does mean being sensitive to people in an organization and utilizing them where they can serve best.

The planners/doers dichotomy is also relevant in understanding the developed structure itself. For example, a youth council formed from within a larger youth group has the function of being the planning group for the larger group. They are not necessarily to do everything, but to plan properly so that things get done. Both planning and doing functions are important, and one of the principles of structuring is to see that both happen.

Structural Nuts and Bolts

One of the major premises of this book is that a solid youth ministry is created from a solid theological foundation. That foundation is grounded in the church, its mission, and the place of youth in it. Therefore, how the youth ministry is structured in *relationship to the church* is also important. Is the youth program separate from the lines of accountability within the church structure? Is there a reporting system to the official church board?

These questions not only reflect lines of responsibility and accountability within a given church structure, but also are ways to live out the mission of the church. As church leaders feel responsible for a youth program, they communicate to their young people support and caring for them as active members. On the other hand, as the youth feel accountable to a formed church body, they begin to learn how to be responsible members of that church. They see their ministry in a larger context and can begin to share in the mission of that church.

It is within this relationship, the give-and-take of responsibility and accountability, that the whole area of financing a youth program needs to be discussed. There are as many methods for financing a youth group as there are churches with youth programs. In a sense, financing needs to be tailored to meet individual congregational situations. However, basically there are only three methods of financing:

1) Through congregational church budget. In this case, the entire youth program for a given period of time becomes an item in the regular budget of the congregation. This is the wholistic approach whereby youth and adults contribute to the church through weekly offerings knowing that their gifts are used to support the total ministry of the church, including ministry with youth. By inclusion in a church budget, the youth program demonstrates its relationship within the broader ministry of a church. A shared ministry is lived out.

2) Through partial congregational support. While some congregations provide thousands of dollars to make possible numerous options and programs for their youth, other churches with more limited financial resources budget for partial program support. The amount may range from tokenism to almost full support; but, in any case, there is only partial congregational support, and the youth themselves must raise the rest of the money. There are various ways this is done: youth offerings received at meetings, charging those who participate in a given program a fee, a system of dues for members, adult individual sponsorship, fund-raising events, or a special congregational appeal. Churches often use a combination of these methods to support their programs.

3) Through total fund-raising or other-than-budget resources. All or any of the possible methods listed under number 2 become the only source of income for the group. Although this financing method may indeed be necessary in

many situations, it is not recommended nor is it the best. First of all, there is no sense of ownership of the youth ministry by a church. A ministry for, with, and by youth is not perceived as a part of the total ministry of the church. Second, there is no active support given by the organized structure of the church. Individuals in any congregation may be totally in favor of youth ministry, but to use an old phrase, "Their money isn't where their mouths are."

How to develop a youth ministry budget depends literally on what it is the group plans to be about. A budget should be a guideline for the program that reflects what is intended in a given period of time. Therefore, it needs to be flexible. It is better to be visionary, leaving room for expansion and experimentation, than to be so pragmatic that there is no space to grow or change. Some possible line items for inclusion in a youth ministry budget might be:

1) Program Expenses
2) Equipment
3) Travel Expenses
4) Youth Leadership Training Events
5) Adult Advisor Training
6) Scholarships (for events or programs outside the congregation)
7) Special Ministry Projects (like shut-in gifts)
8) Benevolence (e.g., supporting an orphan through an interchurch agency)
9) Retreats or Trips

This list is meant to be exemplary, not exhaustive. The items listed and the amounts attached to each should reflect the overall program of the group.

Finally, one of the biggest items of concern in structuring any youth program should be the recognition, channeling, and development of youth leadership. If one of the foundation stones is the recognition that youth are active participants in ministry now, then the place to foster and develop that ministry is in the youth program. The youth-ministry-by-preposition philosophy (youth ministry is ministry *for, with,* and *by* youth) requires a recognition of the development of youth leadership in the doing of its ministry.

Models of Structuring

As stated earlier, a particular organizational structure depends to a large extent on what it is that a group wants to accomplish. There are five basic models and many variations from them. The models are listed here from the most to the least effective.

1) Youth Council or Planning Committee. Called by many different names, this model is representative of the members of the youth group—representative in age, sex, school, geographical area, however diverse the group is. The adult advisors normally also serve on this council. This becomes the planning group for the larger organization. They may not "do" or implement all the planning, but they are responsible for seeing that ideas of the total group are planned.

Sometimes this council is made up of officers, but often there is just a coordinator. There is the need for someone to oversee the entire program. It is hard for a group to be accountable, or, to say it another way, it is too easy for things not to get done when no one is responsible specifically and everyone is generally. It might also be a good idea to assign a member of the church's official board to sit in on this youth council. Lines of communication and a sense of ownership are then developed.

This structure might be diagrammed:

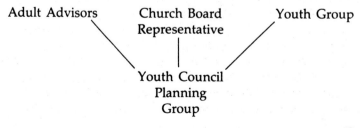

Adult Advisors   Church Board   Youth Group
                        Representative

                        Youth Council
                        Planning
                        Group

The youth council should not be larger than twelve persons because the group will not be able to function well beyond that number. How many advisors and how many youth need to be determined by the youth group itself. One-year terms (running concurrently with the school year) are best. An election process for choosing those persons also tends to develop ownership for the program.

2) Officers. Having elected officers who serve in specific roles for a specified amount of time is another structural model. Sometimes these officers become the youth council as described above. In this model, clear lines of responsibility are delineated. The officers generally include a president, vice-president, secretary, treasurer, and sometimes a chaplain.

This highly structured model works best when a structured program model is used (see next chapter on program models). That is, officers function best in a system where the program varies little and is highly structured. For example, a youth group that meets every Sunday evening and has a program each time which consists of devotions, a business meeting, a program or discussion, and refreshments needs people in specific roles for those meetings. The chaplain has devotions, the president runs the business meeting, and so on.

The strength of this model lies in the fact that roles are specified and clear. The weakness is that persons get pigeonholed, at least for a time. There is a lot of stability, but not much flexibility.

3) Committee of the Whole. Often a group is too small to warrant a complex structure, so the group forms a committee of the whole. Here, the whole youth group is the structure. A coordinator may be elected or officers elected for specific tasks, but everything is done by the whole group.

The strength of this model is that everyone knows what is going on. The problem is that many groups are really too large to operate effectively like this. If the group is over twelve persons, there is need for some other organizational structure. Otherwise, most of the time the group is together will be spent haggling over business and planning and very little may eventually get done.

4) Interest Groups. An interesting concept in youth ministry has been to organize the youth into interest groups. Normally focused around music, drama, or art, these separate interest groups become the youth program for the church. A youth who becomes eligible by age to join the youth group picks an interest group from among the choices offered. Churches that have used this approach have reported a degree of success in attracting youth.

One of the drawbacks to this approach is that there is little diversity of program. Most congregations are not large enough to offer enough creative choices. Therefore, a youth may feel stuck in an interest group he or she does not want and soon quits. Lack of program diversity can lead to a ministry that touches only a few lives (those interested in what is offered) and offers nothing to those who want to experience a broader ministry.

5) Total Adult Coordination. Finally, there is a model for structuring in which the adults do all the programming and make most of the decisions.

Diagrammed, it would look like this:

Adults

|

|

Youth Group

This model represents youth ministry *for* youth, but ignores the possibility of youth ministry *with* and *by* youth. The only time this model might be appropriate would be for purposes of modeling leadership. In other words, where a group needs to learn how to program or how to be good leaders, the adults might serve as living "models" showing how it is done. Since this is appropriate only under that circumstance, it is always a short-term structured model. The quicker youth develop their own leaderships and take ownership for their program in partnership with adult advisors, the better the ministry will develop.

The question of structuring the organization cannot be taken lightly. How one gathers those "two or more" together not only reflects the theological foundation upon which the organization is built; it also affects the program that is to be designed within its structure.

The ground has been dug, a theological foundation laid, a theoretical base developed and structural models for the house proposed. Now, what to do in the house called youth ministry becomes the issue. It is time to explore the actual program itself.

Chapter Five

The Cafeteria vs. the Fast-Food Chain —The Choice of Programming

Three youth were walking down the hall one day at school discussing their church's youth program. They were sharing what their meetings were like.

"We meet every Sunday night," Sara Allison reported. "And at each meeting we have devotions, Bible study, and a business meeting. We're trying to get more kids involved, so we're thinking about changing our meetings. But we don't know what to do. What are the meetings like at your youth group, Sally?"

"They're different each time we go," responded Sally Grosh, a member of a youth group from a neighboring church. "Sometimes we do Bible studies, or have films. Sometimes we go places, or have parties. We don't do the same thing each week. In fact, we don't meet each week. A schedule is sent to us with the date and events. It's never the same but almost always fun."

"Well, I wish our group did something—anything!" Betty Brown chimed in. "We get together, and somebody asks, 'What do you want to do?' and everyone just sits there like dummies. It's really a bore. No one comes anymore because we don't do anything."

These three girls are members of three different youth groups with three different ways of doing things. Their discussion centered around what they did (or did not do) and how often they met. What they were reflecting was their youth "program." "Program" refers to what a group does in a given period of time, usually a school year.

In the case of Betty Brown, the program was one of non-planning. The group gets together, the question is asked: What do you want to do? and if there are suggestions and resources to carry out those suggestions available, the group will try to do it. There is little or no prior planning. Unfortunately, there is little or no program either. This is the extreme case of how not to run a youth program.

The other two girls represent two viable alternatives to youth programming. Each model has its pluses and minuses. Let us examine these two models by use of an analogy.

Nutrition and Choice vs. Quickness and Ease

When choosing a place to eat out, a person has a number of choices. Popular these days are the fast-food restaurants that offer a limited menu, fast service, and reduced prices. There are the not-so-fast places that run from cheap, greasy corner cafes to large, elegant dining halls. Then there is also the cafeteria, where the person has a large number of items to choose from.

Programming for youth ministry can be viewed from this perspective. There are those like the one Sara Allison described, that operate like fast-food restaurants. To coin a phrase, they are the "McDonald's of youth ministry." The accent is on quickness and ease. The program is pretty much the same each time. There are few choices.

The other way was described by Sally Grosh in the opening example. Here, there was program variety, choices, and flexibility. To coin another phrase, this could be called the "cafeteria-style of youth ministry." The focus is on nutrition and choice in what is offered. A balanced program (diet?) is the goal.

These models are meant to be exemplary of the two basic approaches to programming in youth ministry. These models are: (1) the structured program model, and (2) the planning program model. There is that third choice represented by Betty Brown's group—the non-planning, non-program, What-do-you-want-to-do-now? approach. However, since this neither creates nor fosters a solid youth program, there is no sense even discussing it. On the other hand, the two basic programming approaches are viable alternatives.

1) The Structured Program Model. To describe by example is always risky because one tends to overstate or over-generalize. Nevertheless, it may be good to try to picture what this particular model might look like. Sara Allison described it pretty well. The group meets regularly (weekly or biweekly) on a given night during a specified time. Each meeting consists of the same basic elements: opening devotions, business meeting, discussion, or Bible study (or some other intergroup activity), followed by refreshments. The meeting varies usually only at the point of the intergroup activity. The overall program of the youth ministry here is to hold regular, structured meetings as just outlined.

This programming approach has also been called the "canned" approach because of the number of manuals or books that groups use for their meetings. The book becomes the content for the meeting. It tells the group how to do what, when to do it, where, and so on. It is an already prepared program—open the book, read the directions for that particular week's meeting, and do.

The structured program model was the basic style of youth ministry prior to the mid 1960s. Most denominations had youth ministry staffs that provided material (books, manuals, pamphlets) on "what to do on Sunday night with your youth." Very little work needed to be done on the congregational level except to have someone prepare from the book and bring the needed resources together. No one asked if this was what was needed by the group. No one was concerned with addressing needs of youth. The answer to youth ministry was to read and follow "the book."

There are some advantages to this model for programming:
a) *It's quick.* With books and resources easily bought, a

69

program can be put together rather quickly. There is no need to wrestle with the needs-vs.-wants issue. The assumption is that the writer of the book or manual has done that already.

b) *It's easy.* The directions for what to do and how to do it are part of each week's material in the book. Follow the directions, and an evening's activities materialize.

c) *It's comfortable.* Because everything is planned out in the book, there are very few surprises. Everyone knows the format each week, the book plans out the discussion, and everyone knows the outcome of the meetings. There is little spontaneity and very little creativity emerging from the group.

d) *It's inexpensive.* This model is relatively inexpensive to run. A few manuals, some basic resources, a place to meet, a few refreshments (usually donated), and a group has a program.

2) The Planning Program Model. It is clear by now that there is a bias to this book. That bias was stated early and now becomes clearer. Youth ministry is not something that just happens. Furthermore, creative youth ministry takes time and effort. It begins with a theological base, an understanding of youth, a solid theory for development, a structure that supports the program, and a program based on the needs of youth and the mission of the church. "Canned" programs are attempts to develop a program without a major expenditure of time and effort to "build the house."

The bias here is that youth ministry must always take into consideration the local congregational situation. What is right for one congregation may not be right for another. Size, location, identified mission of the church, and youth needs must all be considered in the planning of a youth ministry program. Otherwise, the program becomes youth ministry *for* youth, and the whole prepositional theory of ministry *with* and *by* youth is forgotten.

The structured program model usually begins with the "What" question: What do you want to do? What do we do with the kids? On the other hand, the planning program model begins with asking the deeper questions of "Why?": Why youth ministry? Why should we get together? Then, a program is planned from that basis.

An outline of a planning process follows. It is one of many ways to get at the whole issue of programming. It is an approach that leads to a cafeteria style of nutrition and choice in what is done.

There are four reasons why the planning program model is effective:

a) *It's creative.* Because it is geared to the local congregation and deals with the needs of that particular group, the programming ideas become creative. The secret to effective programming is to be creative, not imitative.

b) *It's varied.* As the group changes with age and new members, so does the program. A solid program for a church tries for balance among its activities and therefore will have a broader appeal for the youth.

c) *It meets needs.* Enough has probably already been said about this. A program designed to meet the needs of those who share in its ministry has a greater chance for growth and meaningfulness.

d) *It's adaptive.* The planning model becomes eclectic, taking ideas from many sources and resources and adapting them to the local situation.

A Planning Process

There are various planning program models from which to choose. The choice of model becomes one of deciding which one suits the purposes and goals of the group using it. The planning process suggested here is one that is easily adaptable to any situation. The process can be used to plan an overall youth program or for individual events within that program. Keep in mind, it is a process—something dynamic, moving, alive. It is also a process that can be used with any structure, for someone still has to decide the how-to's for the group. The planning process is a guide for planning what it is a group needs to do and wants to do. It helps a group be more thorough in its planning.

STEP 1: GATHER DATA

This may seem so obvious that one might not include it in the process, but it is important. Whether planning for a year's worth of activities, or an individual event, there is basic information needed before planning can happen. In a sense, a group needs to reexamine who it is and know something about why it exists. This information includes everything from the quite obvious, such as how many youth are to be involved and their ages, to the not-so-obvious, such as whether the group has goals or purposes for its existence.

Here is an exemplary list of the kinds of information that would be helpful before planning a program for youth ministry:

Why have a youth ministry program? (Someone needs to wrestle with the foundational questions.)

Who wants the program? Who is asking for it?

Who will sponsor the program? (A complex question that gets into the whole area of adult advisors and finances.)

Who will participate in the program? (Age, sex ratio, school representation, economic levels, etc.)

What are the pressures that may affect participation? (Money, age, school functions, time pressures, etc.)

What is the goal or purpose of the organization? (One of the first things a group needs is an identifiable purpose for its existence; perhaps a program gets planned by starting here first.)

Another whole area for data collection is that of the needs, values, and interests of those who will participate. Chapter 3 dealt with some of those values and interests as they apply to youth generally; but as a specific program is developed locally, it would be good to gather specific information from the prospective participants. One way to do this is with an *interest finder*. Consider some possible questions to ask:

1) The basics—name, address, grade in school, sex, phone, age, school attending, church membership.
2) Church involvement—participation in things like worship, church school, acolyte, usher, lector, choir, other areas of service.
3) What events would you like to see offered during this next year?
4) What are some of the biggest issues, interests, or concerns you have?
5) What are the best times for meeting?

If there was time and the planning group saw the need for it, a more thorough form of questionnaire could be used that would get at values and needs even more directly. There is not enough space to develop an example fully here, but if a group desires to do so, they can develop a survey on their own. Creativity can go a long way toward developing energy and enthusiasm for a developing program. Simply ask, What is it we need to know? and go from there.

Gathering data does not have to be time consuming, for most of the information needed is already at hand. However, it is important not to neglect even the obvious because it could have an effect on the program. One example would be if a group of junior-high girls serving as a planning group decided to have a dance. If the entire group is made up of 95 percent girls and 5 percent bashful, shy junior-high boys, there may be a problem. Outside boys may need to be "imported" to balance the sexes better. The point here is that someone must take a look at all the possibilities in the planning process. Data gathering is the first step.

STEP 2: ANALYZE THE DATA

Once the data have been collected, the next step is to examine them. Raw information is not helpful unless someone analyzes and interprets it. Depending upon how

73

much has been collected, the first step in analysis is to sort out the data received.

Here are some basic questions that can be asked:

What do the data say?

What are the givens—people, time, place, resources?

What are the primary needs expressed?

What are the suggestions that keep coming up?

What are the implications for planning?

This step may not take much time either, but it needs to be thoughtfully covered. If a group just getting started is possibly going to be large in numbers, there had better be a large enough space to hold that first gathering. The implications for planning in analyzing the data are significant, and someone must do it.

STEP 3: DEVELOP A STATEMENT OF SPECIFIC OBJECTIVES

Now that the data have been gathered and analyzed, what is it that the group wants to do? Unfortunately, this is the question that most groups start with, but it is appropriate only at this point in the planning process. If the group has already thought through and formulated a purpose statement for the organization itself, the next step is to develop a statement or statements of specific objectives. Again, this planning step is applicable whether you are planning a whole year's program or a single event.

The specific objectives outline what is to happen with the participants in light of the data gathered. The most helpful objectives should meet the SCAMP criteria:

S – Specific: Objectives must be very specific and concrete.

(example: To involve thirty-five young people in our youth ministry this next year.)

C – Consistent: They must fit into the overall purpose of the organization.

(example: To participate in a Bible

		study retreat designed to explore what discipleship means.)
A –	Attainable:	The objectives should be things that can be done. (example: To make gifts for our shut-in members at Christmastime.)
M –	Measurable:	The objectives should be written so that they can be evaluated. (example: To plan and conduct two special worship services for the congregation.)
P –	Personal:	There must be something that each member of the group can become involved in and be willing to explore.

STEP 4: DEVELOP A GENERAL PLAN OR OVERALL DESIGN

To stay with the analogy of building a house, we now need to construct a framework. The overall layout of the rooms or the general format of the inside needs to be put in place. Using the planning process to this point, it is now time to develop a brief, capsule picture of the program. This helps to get a sense of the flow and balance of what will hopefully be done.

This step is an outline, broadly constructed, of the program being planned, whether that program is a whole year of youth ministry activities or a one-night event. By making this overall design, it is possible to step back from it and to get the whole picture in perspective. In examining this general plan, it would be good to look for three qualities: (1) *Unity. Do all parts help to meet the purpose of the organization? Do all parts of the design match with one or more of the specific objectives?* (2) *Flow.* Does the total program have a certain movement to it? Is that movement one that builds and gives a degree of momentum to the group? Do the transitions within the program contribute to the flow? (3) *Balance.* Is there adequate program

75

balance so that various interests and needs are met? (More will be said on balance under Program Principles later in this chapter.)

It is also important at this point in the process to examine where the program, or the major portions of it, will take place. The facilities and meeting place are part of the atmosphere. This atmosphere can help or hinder the unity, flow, and balance of any design. A good design also strives to control the "climate" for where a group meets. For a lively activity, bright lights and a lot of space are needed. For an evening of small-group discussion, more subdued lighting and more intimate meeting areas are needed. Good planning will strive to use the setting to the best advantage to meet the purpose and objectives.

A possible way to develop a general plan or overall design would be to use the following steps:

1) List each specific objective and rank them in order of importance for the group.
2) Brainstorm all the options to help meet each objective. (These are specific activities that will satisfy the objective.)
3) Sort out the brainstormed list, combining, eliminating, or adding those items helpful in meeting the specific objectives.
4) Arrange a brief outline for the program planned. (This could be an outline of a year's youth ministry program, a part of a year, or one event.)

A word about brainstorming may be in order. This is possibly the single most important activity any group engages in. Brainstorming is the process of listing as many ideas as possible, as fast as possible. During the process there should be no evaluation or comment on the ideas suggested. Every idea is accepted and listed in the brainstorming activity. Comments and clarification of ideas come later.

There are six general rules for brainstorming:

1) Express no evaluation. Every idea is accepted.

2) Work for quantity. The longer the list gets, the more likely it will contain some really workable and useful ideas.

3) Expand on others' ideas. There is a triggering effect as one person's ideas trigger ideas in others.

4) Encourage the far-out ideas. This opens the door for creativity, individuality, the unusual, and helps people see things in new ways.

5) Record each idea. This is essential so that no ideas are lost.

6) Set a time limit. A time limit will increase the commitment and the energy of the persons involved. The amount of time needed will vary according to the item being brainstormed.

The use of brainstorming and the adherence to the rules help groups to be creative and to think in new ways. A large volume of ideas gets generated. Ideas and germs of ideas are permitted to grow and develop. Group problem solving then becomes a cooperative venture that builds community.

STEP 5: DEVELOP SPECIFIC STRATEGIES, ACTIVITIES, OR EVENTS

Using the specific objectives from step 3 and the overall design from step 4 (including the brainstormed ideas), it is time to prepare the details of the program or event. These details include the preparation needed, the follow-up steps, and the plan for implementation. Ask the following questions about each part of the program:

What will be done?

How will it be done?

When will it be done?

How much time will it take?

Who is responsible for preparation?

Who is responsible for leadership?

What resources are required?

It may be helpful to develop some kind of planning sheet for a program or event. In this way, all the essentials are covered and the people involved get a sense of ownership for what is being planned. It is also a good practice to write this planning down so that people know specific responsibilities for an event or program.

As specific events are being planned, it might be good to explore where ideas for programs can be acquired. Where does a group start to get ideas for its programs? In other words, how does a group answer the question that is now appropriately asked: Well, what do you want to do? Here are five suggestions:

1) Start with the youth themselves. Brainstorm ideas. Watch and listen as a group discusses: What are their major concerns? What annoys them most? What do they like? Dislike? How do they have fun? What's happening in school? At home? What's lacking in their lives?

2) Where is the most controversy? Where there are heated differences of opinion, that is where the most under-standing, growing, and healing can occur.

3) Listen to the prophets of today and yesterday. Keep open to those persons who speak with a conscience prodded by God. Listen to the music of today, the poetry and writers that youth read. Here is a great opportunity to respond as these prophets touch the conscience of youth.

4) Keep a file of ideas. Include everything that might someday be usable. This file could include: topics; questions; Bible studies; newspaper and magazine articles; a list of resource books, films, speakers, games, retreats, records, role-plays, and places to go.

5) Always involve the total group in developing ideas. A greater sense of ownership and responsibility is fostered as everyone participates.

STEP 6: EVALUATE

A careful analysis or review needs to be done after the program or event has been completed. All elements or parts that helped create the experience need to be evaluated. Strengths and weaknesses are examined constructively in order to make improvements in planning or leadership for the future. Evaluation should include looking at such areas as understandings, emotions, skill competency, group process, future training, program design, leadership, and learnings.

The planning process is a systematic way to help any group organize what it needs and wants to do. The model described works for planning a single event or a whole program of various events. It is important to remember that a process is only as good as those who use it. The more it is used, the easier it gets; and soon planning becomes second nature in creating a solid youth ministry.

Program Principles—The Diamond

How is a church youth program different from the youth program of any other organization? That is a question worthy of comment. The obvious answer is that a youth program sponsored by a church has a base in the theology and ministry of that church. Youth ministry becomes part of the message and mission of the church's life. So far, so good. No one can quibble with that answer to this point.

Unfortunately, there is a problem when one actually examines the program and events of some church youth ministries. They may be tied to the church by sponsorship, but their programs bear no resemblance whatsoever to the message and mission of the church. Some programs that pass for youth ministry are nothing more than organized social clubs or recreational groups. The relationship to the church is in name only.

The quality of balance becomes crucial in addressing this issue. For youth ministry to be part of the ministry of a church, those who are part of it must see themselves as

79

bearers of the message of Christ and participants in the mission of his church. The place where this is demonstrated is in the program itself. What kind of balance is there in the activities being planned? Is everything fun and games? Are all programs "Sunday schoolish" in character? How do youth serve in the church?

A balanced program includes activities of various kinds that meet the needs of youth, hold their interest, and live out the mission of the church. The *Programming Diamond* is a good principle to keep in mind while designing a total youth ministry program.

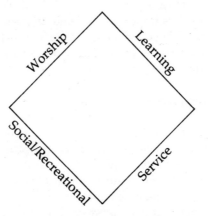

The four parts of the diamond correspond to the four functions of the church discussed in chapter 2, i.e., worship, teach, witness, and serve. Any good youth program will strive to strike a balance among the four types of activities. A group that does nothing but have recreational events is not only forgetting its mission to serve; it also will not attract those who are neither interested in nor good at sports. The balancing principle in programming helps the people in the youth ministry group to live out its relationship to the church as well as to attract and meet the needs of a larger group of youth.

80

It is possible to examine the overall program for a youth group and to evaluate it in terms of balance. Some activities that a group does can meet more than one of the parts of the diamond. For example, a Bible study which combines a devotional period with a plan to actually live out what was studied can meet three parts of the diamond. The better the program is balanced, the better the chances for eliminating the roller-coaster effect described in the last chapter. A balanced program leads to greater continuity.

How a Group Becomes a Group

This chapter would be seriously incomplete without addressing the question of group development. All the planning in the world will not guarantee cohesiveness to people who come together to form a group. Not even a well-balanced program is a guarantee of that happening. The question needs to be asked: How does a group become a group? What are the factors or elements important in group formation and development? As one youth advisor noted: "We plan the best meetings we can, but nothing seems to happen. Everyone is quiet and shy. Our best-planned meetings die." Why? It is very simple—attention has not been paid to some basic elements of group development.

Whenever people gather together to form a group, there are a few basic concerns that need to be dealt with before people will feel comfortable. From a systematic study of hundreds of groups of all shapes and sizes, from both business and social organizations, Jack Gibb, a social scientist, has worked out a theoretical model which provides one way of looking at the basic concerns as people form into a group.

The four major concerns are: 1) Acceptance; 2) Data-flow; 3) Goal formation; 4) Control (or leadership)

1) *Acceptance.* This is the question of membership in the group. The person wrestling with this concern is asking:

"Who am I in this group? What will it cost me to belong?" If this concern goes unresolved, fear and mistrust are evident. When a person feels a part of the group, acceptance and trust can be seen. This element of concern for acceptance is crucial in youth ministry. Until the youth feel accepted by those in the group, there will be a lot of fear which shows itself in quietness or shyness. If the youth just sit around in small cliques and will not relate to others, group acceptance needs to be developed. This is true in youth ministry because of the disparity of ages and schools, and because one of the personal issues confronting teens is the identity search (discussed in chapter 3). Somehow, youth need to feel accepted for who they are. When that happens, trust can begin forming.

2) *Data-Flow.* This concern represents the other side of the membership question. The concern may be expressed by these questions: Who else is here? What status do the other members have here? Who has what weight in decision-making?

What is called for is data-flow, or interpersonal sharing. The people in the group need to get to know one another. The mistake in youth ministry is to assume that because youth may go to the same school or are the same age or sing in the choir together that they know one another. A group that wants to live out its life as part of the ministry of the church needs to be concerned with ministry to its members. Knowing the other person (in biblical terms, recognizing my neighbor) is critical for trust to develop and a group to take on identity.

3) *Goal Formation.* This is the concern for productivity represented by the questions: Why are we here? What can we do together? As people gain a sense of the purpose for the group, they can choose either to buy in or not to be a part. As people in youth ministry accept and formulate their purposes (based on theological and solid principles), everyone can discover what part they can play in the program.

4) *Control (or Leadership)*. This is the concern for organization and structure: How are we going to accomplish our goal? What procedures shall we use? Who is going to do what? Shared leadership and interdependence among group members becomes the goal as these questions are dealt with.

The Gibb Theory is applicable to any group and is therefore relevant to youth ministry. By understanding the various concerns as group trust is developed, a group can go in new directions with its programming. For example, a group that has trouble getting discussions started perhaps ought to examine the group development stages and see where their group is having its problem. If the members of the group are afraid to relate, some nonthreatening games that get them to interact may be necessary. It may take as long as a year for a group of teens to feel comfortable enough with one another (perhaps longer with adults) to discuss important subjects or to engage in in-depth Bible study. Good programming will recognize the concerns of the group as it forms and will strive to address those concerns constructively.

Basic Planning Principles

The choice of programming is an important decision in youth ministry. The planning becomes as important as the doing. What to do and how it is done are reflections of the base and groundwork developed. Here are some basic planning principles that are important to keep in mind as programming is reflected on:

1) Seek balance.
2) Use the talents and skills of the members of the group.
3) Keep in mind that it is impossible to meet all the needs of all the people. (The cafeteria style does the best job.)
4) Be creative. This will keep the group dynamic, changing, and relevant.
5) Be intentional about developing relationships in the group. Strive to live out the gospel of love and forgiveness with those who share in the ministry.

The house called youth ministry has been created. Models for what to do in the house have been offered, and some hints about planning have been suggested. It is time to examine who is going to staff that house. The important role of youth advisors now becomes the issue for examination.

Chapter Six
The Big Kids
—The Youth Advisors

The church council members of Advent Church were planning to restart their youth program. It had been four years since the Garmans had announced they would no longer serve as youth advisors. Everyone on the council was in agreement that the youth of Advent needed a new program. However, the discussion centered around who should be the advisors.

"I still say we should hire a seminarian," said Harry Brumbach, repeating his earlier statement. "They are young, would probably relate well to the kids, the experience would be good for them, and we would be sure to get a good program. After all, volunteers never work as well as paid staff."

"Why not ask the Cavanaughs?" asked Julie Newman. "They are a young couple with no children. I'm sure they would have the time, and they would be good with kids."

Bill Jacobs reached back into the past. "When we were in youth group, our parents were the advisors, and it worked pretty well. If the kids want a program, have them get their parents involved."

"I don't care who we get," added Mary Steiner, "but it should be someone responsible whom the kids will relate to."

"Maybe we should put an announcement in our church newsletter that we're looking for someone to be a youth advisor," suggested Sam Williams. "That way we won't waste our time asking people who aren't interested, and those who would inquire would already be showing their interest."

The discussion at Advent Church was not an unusual one. Their interest was in finding the best persons to serve the church in the youth program. Their suggested solutions to the problem reflect the various options open to a congregation as they wrestle with this issue. None of the solutions are wrong, but they are not all effective ones.

This chapter deals with "staffing the house." Who makes the most effective youth advisor? How does a congregation find these people? What are the roles and expectations for those who would serve? These are the pertinent questions when considering youth advisors.

Perhaps a word needs to be said at the beginning regarding the title for adults who serve in youth ministry. There are many titles used: counselor, youth worker, youth director, advisor. This book has consistently used the term "youth advisor" or "advisor" as the designated title. This is intentional. Of all the titles used, the one of youth advisor best serves the prepositional philosophy of youth ministry proposed by this book. "Counselor" has a formal flavor to it connoting a ministry that goes "to" youth. "Director" implies a leadership role of running the program—again, a philosophy of going to youth. "Youth worker" is a bland term that hints of a ministry "with" youth and a partnership, but there is no sense of adult role in that. "Youth advisor" is more a term that easily identifies the person as an adult in a consultative role. This allows for ministry "for," "with," and "by" youth, which correlates to the philosophy proposed.

All the titles are certainly usable and indeed are used throughout the churches of this country. Thought should be given to the title, however, as it conveys something of the role expectation of the person who bears it.

Various Congregational Styles

The discussion at Advent Church described fairly clearly three of the four congregational models that are widely used with regard to youth advisors. As stated earlier, there are no right or wrong ways to staff a youth program. The concern is to have persons serve who are responsible and responsive to the youth. Some models or styles are more effective than others, however.

1) *The Team Approach* (four or more adults). This is one model not proposed by the Advent council but one that could have happened had they used Sam's suggestion of advertising for persons to serve. Of all the models possible, this one has the greatest chances for effectiveness. How to establish this approach in terms of recruitment (Sam's suggestion) will be discussed later.

The team approach is one in which four or more adults serve as advisors to a youth group. There are some obvious strengths to this. First of all, the responsibility is spread among more persons, thus no one or two people feel the whole weight for the program resting with them. Shared leadership is modeled by the advisors each having a part in the total program. Second, the more persons involved, the greater diversity of gifts and talents available for the group. Four committed adults obviously bring a wider range of skills and backgrounds than does a single adult advisor. This can lead to greater program possibilities and to a more balanced approach to programming. Instead of relying on the interests and skills of one adult, the group has more resources to draw from. Third—and related to the second advantage—with the team approach, more adult models or examples are available to the youth. Not only is the program enriched by more adults, the youth themselves have more opportunities to see and experience the Christian life lived out in the lives of the adults they work with. This is one of the ways the theological base for providing youth ministry gets demonstrated (refer to chapter 2, "Why Youth Ministry?") in providing for significant models of the Christian life.

The team approach does have some potential dangers. If the team gets too large, there is the possibility of adult domination of both the program and of the group itself. A proper balance needs to be kept, and those on the team need to be clear about their role as advisors. The other potential danger has to do with the internal workings of the team itself. The more people, the more need there is for clearer lines of communication and openness. There is always the danger of conflicting styles, philosophies, and interests which could adversely affect the whole youth ministry program. Those who serve on a team must be committed to the team approach and to those with whom they serve. An intentional team ministry will start with everyone's understanding and accepting the philosophy of youth ministry that serves as the basis for that ministry to happen.

2) *A Young Couple.* Julie Newman suggested that Advent Church would be served well by the Cavanaughs, whom she described as "a young couple" who would "have the time" and "would be good with kids." This is not an unusual congregational answer to the question, Who will be good youth advisors? Indeed, it is a logical suggestion and one that works for many congregations. A young couple who have interest in youth and have the time to serve can be good advisors because age-wise they are close to the youth and are not identified by youth as parents or parent-role people. There is normally easy rapport established as well as common bonds created through mutual interests. For example, young adults are able to participate in physical activities like roller skating or volleyball easier than adults of older generations.

The main problems with this model are that it places an extreme amount of responsibility and expectations on two people and that there are only two persons whose resources can be tapped. A young couple serving as youth advisors also tend to burn themselves out and lose interest in the group much quicker if they serve by themselves rather than on a team. The mutual stimulation and encouragement of other adults are often missing in this style.

3) *A Bright Young Person.* When Harry Brumbach sug-

gested hiring a seminarian in the role of advisor, he was demonstrating this particular congregational model. It is not always a seminarian who is hired, but the model is to "hire" a bright young person who will relate well to the youth. The lines of responsibility and accountability are supposedly ensured through the hiring principle. Unfortunately, this model is rarely effective.

First of all, the whole program is on the shoulders of one person. The buck stops with that person, and there is normally a high level of "success orientation." The young person hired wants to prove his or her competency. However, the expectations are rarely realistic or clear. Second, the person hired is normally not a member of the congregation. In a sense, the congregation farms out its youth ministry program. Because the person is brought in, he or she is relatively unfamiliar with the congregation and therefore directs the planning process in a vacuum. Finally, because the expectations are high in hiring a bright, energetic young person, immediate results are anticipated. The leadership model of the young person has the tendency to become authoritarian, and the ministry can become directed "to" the youth, rather than in partnership with them. Church councils want to see results—increased numbers of youth and more activities. The means to accomplish those ends can be ignored, and therefore the ministry can lose its focus and ignore its real reason for existence, namely for, with, and by the youth themselves.

If a congregation does choose to hire someone, the best thing that person can do is to coordinate the establishment of a team of volunteer advisors. The accountability is still there, as the hired person is responsible to the governing body for the program, but the responsibility gets shared. All the other benefits of a team approach also become evident.

4) *Parents*. Bill Jacobs at Advent Church believed that parents of the youth involved should be the advisors. The argument for this model usually goes something like this: "If

the youth and their parents want a youth program, they should be the ones to do it. It can lead to greater family unity and they are the logical choices."

Reflecting back to chapter 3 and the characteristics of the adolescent years, it will be noted that the search for identity and independence are two of the struggles of teens. These struggles are directly related to family and parental environment. Youth need to find themselves and develop a value system which is theirs separate from the values of parents. This does not mean the values will be noticeably different. It does mean that the search must be done with a degree of independence. One of the places that search is helped is in the church. A solid youth ministry offers models and examples of Christians who live out their faith in many ways. Having parents serve as advisors limits the chance of that search for their youth.

There is also the very likely possibility of parental misunderstandings and interference if parents are involved. Someone is bound to comment about favoritism. The whole program can lose objectivity if that happens.

Again, the place where parents may be involved is on a team approach where there are other adult advisors who are not parents of the youth involved. There are more Christian models available, and youth themselves may feel freer to relate to other adults. The responsibility is shared and therefore the danger of favoritism in dealing with the youth is minimized.

A word about recruiting advisors would be in order at this point. In the story about Advent Church, Sam Williams suggested a notice in the church newsletter to attract interested persons. Although this may be a way to publicize the need for advisors, it is rarely a good method for finding any. First, volunteering for anything is not a socially acceptable thing to do. Many adults are scared to death of teen-agers and would not even consider the possibility of serving their church as adult advisors to a youth program. Therefore, those adults would probably read right over a newsletter announcement without a personal thought to themselves. There is also the tendency to read such an announcement and to never personally consider their own response to that need. Someone else is always thought of as being the right person for the job.

Second, trying to recruit through indirect appeal will not guarantee the best people for the role. Sam was right in that truly interested people would respond, but that does not make them the most effective advisors possible.

There is only one way to adequately acquire the best persons to serve as youth advisors—go after them directly and personally. Look around the congregation and see who are the most likely people to make effective advisors. Make a list of names. Think through the qualities needed for the given situation. Then, seek those people out personally and challenge them with the opportunity to serve. Tell them why they are being asked, what is involved in the role, and what the expectations are. Let them know what qualities they possess that make them right for the job. This is the only effective way to do recruitment—intentionally and personally.

Expectations of Youth Advisors

It is only fair that when a person takes on a responsibility he or she is aware of the expectations. What is it that is to be done? What kind of time commitment can be expected? What are the various parts of the job itself?

Although the amount of time commitment called for will vary with the situation as well as the specific jobs to be done, an illustrative list of expectations can be drawn up here as an example. The youth advisor would be expected to:

1) work directly with the young people in the group;
2) assist the youth council (or program planning group) in program and event planning;

3) continue to maintain and develop a working philosophy and theology of youth ministry for the church;
4) be concerned with the personal growth and development of young people;
5) be an example (model) of the church in action;
6) attend at least one training workshop per year;
7) be responsible, with the youth, to the governing body of the congregation for the youth ministry program;
8) be a mature adult—open and flexible to new ideas and yet clear about his or her role in the group as an adult.

Any such list of expectations should be developed by those persons to whom the youth advisor is accountable. A clear set of expectations can lead to a more objective evaluation and appraisal of the person who agrees to do the job. Since these expectations would be clear from the start, there would be no surprises when it is time to evaluate the advisors. This is the only fair way both to recruit someone for the position and to evaluate the person once he or she is in it.

Roles of Youth Advisors

Youth advisors are also expected to play a number of roles as responsibility for the youth group is assumed. These roles are identified as the givens in a youth group situation. The youth advisor is cast into the roles, like it or not, by virtue of being the advisor.

1) *Leadership Role.* Like it or not, the youth advisor is one of the leaders of the group. The youth will look to the advisor for help in setting the direction for the group. Notice that the advisor is *one* of the leaders. In youth ministry, effective leadership is shared leadership. The youth advisor helps develop and nurture the leadership qualities from within the group itself.

There is also the serious responsibility of seeing that the whole program is consistent with the theology and philosophy of youth ministry for the church. The youth advisor as leader helps to see that the program is balanced and that what is done is consistent with what should be done as a part of the Church of Jesus Christ.

2) *Modeling vs. Christian Cloning.* A distinction needs to be made between setting an example (or being a model) and being a manufacturer of Christians, what could be called Christian cloning. The Christian life takes many shapes, forms, and sizes. The gifts of the Holy Spirit given to the people who are the body of Christ are diverse and many. Care must be taken not to assume the attitude that all young people must think, feel, and act exactly like us or they are not Christian.

There are many models for the Christian way of life, just as there are many models and types of planes in the sky. All of them fly. All of them do what they are created to do, but they come in many shapes and sizes. Being a model that young people can respect is an important role, but turning out more people who are exactly like others is not the way to do it. In fact, if all persons in a group were alike it would be boring. Christian cloning, making photocopies of adults, is not the goal of youth ministry. Helping young people develop, grow, and mature as responsible Christians is. This happens through good modeling.

3) *Stabilizing Role.* In youth ministry, things change rapidly. Every year the youth involved get one year older and one year more mature. New people are constantly joining the group bringing new interests and skills with them. As new people come in, the complexity of the group changes. There needs to be some stabilizing force that brings a measure of consistency and continuity to the group. That force can be the youth advisor.

This does not mean being rigid. The youth advisor should be free and flexible, willing to try new things, discover new directions with the group. However, as the group changes, there needs to be solid ground on which to build. Someone should know the history and be aware of the roots of the organization. A degree of continuity is important so that those who are part of the group can learn what the expectations of their youth group are. The advisor is in the best position to serve in that role.

Leadership Styles—A Prepositional Approach

There are three basic styles of leadership. These styles are meant to be descriptive of how a person functions or sees himself or herself functioning in a group. Therefore, as descriptive styles, they are not judgments about what is right or wrong. None of the styles is all right or all wrong. In fact, no adult leader will use one style all the time or in all circumstances. It is true that each person has a dominant style. However, the key to effective adult leadership lies in finding a style that is comfortable for the leader and effective with the group. Different circumstances and situations call for different styles. A good youth advisor will be aware of the style he or she is operating in and should be able to assess the success of that style both for himself or herself personally and for the group. Being aware of the different styles and evaluating personal styles and situations, a youth advisor is in a good position to make conscious decisions regarding the uses of the various styles. An effective youth advisor will be able to adapt and change styles as situations warrant.

These three leadership styles can be examined by a prepositional approach:

1) *In.* In this style, the leader is *in the center* of the group. All activity and planning revolve around the leader. This is also known as the *authoritative* style of leadership. In this style, the adult generally makes the decisions, and the youth of the group participate in plans decided for them. The control for the entire group rests with the leader. Everyone looks to the leader for the answers to questions or problems, for suggestions and ideas about what to do, and even for directions on how to do them. Youth are involved primarily in the doing of the activities, rather than in the planning of them.

The authoritative style should not be confused with authoritarian behavior. The style is simply a way to identify who is in charge. It is traditionally the style assumed by most youth advisors and is still used by many in youth ministry today.

2) *With.* There is a style of leadership that can be identified as the leader *with the group.* This is also known as the *participatory* style. It is the style which involves the adult working in partnership with the youth in both the planning and the doing aspects of the program. Decisions and responsibilities are shared.

This model or style assumes that no one person has all the answers to all the questions and that it is in the group working together that the answers can be creatively found. The adult sees himself or herself as a person among other persons, some of them youth. The adult believes that neither age nor experience are the essentials in developing a program of ministry for, with, and by youth. In the participatory style, the value of each person and the contribution that each can make are extremely important.

3) *Out.* The third style of leadership can be described as the leader *out of the group.* This style is also called *Laissez Faire,* which means "let do." In this style, the adult assumes a position outside of the group itself. When called upon for help or advice, he or she is available, but at all other times, the youth are allowed to function as they wish. The direction for planning and programming of the group is set solely by the youth. The youth advisor does not offer input of any kind unless asked to do so by the youth of the group. This style assumes a hands-off attitude and approach in which the adult functions only as a consultant and only when consulted.

As stated before, none of the styles is all right or all wrong. Every person in a leadership role usually forms a dominant style which is used most frequently. The secret to effectiveness is learning what style works best with the group. This is another good argument for a team approach for youth advisors. The team approach allows for greater variety of leadership styles and serves not only to demonstrate different styles but also to keep any one style from becoming *the* style for a group.

Characteristics of Effective Youth Advisors

Dr. Merton P. Strommen, in his book *Five Cries of Youth*, revealed the results of research he did with identified persons throughout the United States who are outstanding leaders with youth. The survey represented a large denominational mixture. The most interesting of the results dealt with the issue of how effective leaders approach youth. The questions asked were: What ways of approaching youth have you found helpful? and How do you get next to them? The responses revealed six groups of skills exercised by these successful church youth workers. Examples of how to apply that skill were listed under each group of skills.

1) Building Relationships
>   Knowing them—home life, school, friends.
>   Exhibiting deep, sensitive, personal concern for them.
>   Showing them courtesy.
>   Participating with them as an equal.
>   Showing appreciation for a job well done.
>   Helping them if they ask.
>   Sharing mutual experiences.
>   Sharing my own feelings about life.

2) Being Genuine
>   Being adult.
>   Speaking in my own vocabulary.
>   Being honest and open.
>   Stating my convictions while leaving room for theirs.
>   Boldly speaking out in radical situations.

Admitting I don't know all the answers.

Dealing with my own hang-ups first.

3) Being Available

Going to their events when adults are welcome.

Spending time with them and their friends.

Working and playing with them in various activities.

Taking kids to "away" games.

Picking up hitchhikers.

Inviting them to my home for dinner.

Initiating interviews.

4) Showing Interest

Remembering their names.

Learning about their world.

Being able to speak their language.

Listening to their music.

Adopting their symbols.

Finding areas where I can be of help.

Phone calls and letters regarding their accomplishments and interests.

5) Communicating

Talking to them every opportunity I get.

Slow, quiet listening; waiting for the chance to say some things.

Listening with the third ear for emotions.

One-to-one counseling.

6) Leading

Discovering and using their talents and interests.

Involving them in planning, decision-making, and executing activities.

Letting them find their own thing and do it.

Accepting their decisions.

Facing them with the issues.

Holding unpopular positions which I think are best for them.

Giving them provocative, challenging books.

Offering them a host of options.

Presenting a better alternative by the way I live and act.

Getting them interested in trips, projects, studies to benefit them.

Creating celebration and experiences for free expressions.

Taking them to camps, retreats.

Next, Strommen asked these leaders: What are you doing to accomplish (your) purposes (with youth)? Three new groups of skills were revealed:

7) Teaching

Training others to reach out on a one-to-one basis.

Training leaders to program "exposure events."

Reeducating adults to helping roles with youth.

Teaching the Scriptures, presenting verbally and nonverbally the message of Christ.

Teaching a class relating Bible, youth, and culture.

Personally confronting each youth with the claims of Christ.

Relating youth's ideas to Christian faith.

8) Creating a Community

Helping them to get to know one another.

Encouraging group awareness and sensitivity in everyday life.

Finding Christ in one another, in everyone we encounter, in everything we do.

Through involvement, make them aware of loneliness, deprivation, friendlessness.

Helping forgiveness and acceptance to happen.

Developing teamwork among youth in their activities.

Trying to build a staff community.

Developing groups who share at the deepest possible level.

Keeping the group open to friends of church youth.

9) Encouraging Involvement

Involving kids where they can grow, experience, relate, share—volunteer work, seminars, schools, inner city, community.

Going to another community or culture for service projects.

Getting young people into the establishment.

Creating opportunities for kids to think about, talk about, and act out their own concerns.

Discussing issues and trying to do something about them.[1]

It should be clear by now that the skills mentioned are really outgrowths of what it means to be an effective youth advisor. The examples given under the nine skills are illustrative of how some of these leaders have done it. They are ways of living the Gospel, of putting flesh on the theological foundations of chapter 2, of responding to who youth are and what they need. However, keep in mind that these are only examples. No one person is expected to be everything to everyone. These examples represent the ideal. There are no such animals as superhuman youth advisors. There *are* a lot of people who are committed, caring, and interested in youth.

Dr. Stommen summarized it best when he boiled everything down to two imperatives in youth ministry— *mutuality and mission.* "Youth of all subcultures want the warmth of an accepting group which is *mutuality.* They need activities which give them a sense of purpose; that is *mission.* Within these two polarities, there is powerful need for educational experiences for youth and adults that open minds, develop skills, clarify values, and encourage commitment."[2] The youth advisor has a home in helping to meet that need.

The house called youth ministry has been solidly built. As the foundation was laid, there was room for creativity and uniqueness as a congregation strove to build its house on its location in its own way. Now it is time for some embellishments. These are the little extras that give the house flavor and character of its own.

Chapter Seven

The Little Items That Pay Big Dividends
—Administrative Ideas

The vestry of St. Paul's Church was beginning to gather for their monthly meeting. Over in the corner, Jack, Tom, and Martha were discussing an announcement in last Sunday's bulletin that intrigued them. The announcement read: "SPY is coming. Keep an eye out for more clues."

"What do you think SPY is?" Jack asked. "I don't remember any vestry discussion about anything that sounded like it."

"I'll bet it's some musical group coming in," Martha speculated. "You know how the pastor loves to be creative with his announcements."

"Let's ask the pastor when he comes," suggested Tom. "There are a lot of people who have asked me about it, figuring that since I was on the vestry I would know. There are a lot of people as curious as we are about it."

"What do you suppose it means?" reflected Jack, again.

Just then, Pastor Wilson came into the room. He moved freely and easily among the vestry members greeting each by name and saying a few words to everyone. Pastor Wilson had come to St. Paul's Church less than a year ago. He was a dynamic, creative leader and was well liked.

When he got to the place where Jack, Tom, and Martha were standing, he was greeted by Tom, who immediately asked the question, "Pastor, what did last week's bulletin announcement about 'SPY is coming' mean? What is SPY?"

Pastor Wilson laughed. "I see our announcement made people curious. I'm glad. I am going to inform the vestry, but

I'll let you in on the secret now. Remember two months ago when we decided that St. Paul's should start up its youth program again?"

They all nodded their heads that they remembered the discussion.

"Well, you asked me to try to locate capable advisors and to get the group going," continued Pastor Wilson. "I've been working pretty hard on this. I have five advisors now, and we sat down last week to see how we can interest the kids into coming to a meeting. Jane Lyson came up with the bulletin idea to whet everyone's appetite."

"You mean," interrupted Jack, "that the announcement was about the new youth group?"

"Right," Pastor Wilson affirmed, "SPY is an anagram that stands for St. Paul's Youth. In later bulletin announcements we will reveal this, but for now we want to arouse interest and curiosity. It looks like it's working."

"It sure is," commented Tom. "None of us had any idea."

"I think it's a great idea," Martha reflected. "It has everyone guessing and will surely interest our youth."

Jack thought for a second then added, "SPY, huh? That sure fooled me. I like it."

If the example of Trinity Church from chapter 1 can stand as a model of how *not* to start a youth program, the example of St. Paul's can be a model of how to *creatively* start one. Although there are many ways to start groups, St. Paul's has discovered one of the best.

What makes their example such a good one? There are a number of reasons. First of all, the decision to start a youth ministry began with the vestry, or official board. They felt responsible and during a discussion the pastor was asked to give his impetus to getting the group started. Second, the pastor took an active role in organizing. There are many pastors who claim that with all the other responsibilities they have, they do not have the time to do this. It is true that the demands on a pastor's time and energy are great. However, the reality is that he or she needs to show active interest. Any church with an active youth program will also be a church where the pastor shows more than casual interest in the group. This does not mean that the more involved the pastor is, the better the group. It does mean that a pastor's participation and involvement are important, especially as a youth ministry gets started. Third, the curiosity of the whole congregation was aroused. As the reactions of Jack, Tom, and Martha showed, when the word gets out about what SPY stands for, there is going to be great interest in the program. Finally, the group began with a name. More will be said on this later in the chapter.

St. Paul's was on its way to developing a creative youth ministry. Certainly, foundations need to be laid, a theology formulated, and a working philosophy developed; but there is time to do that as the group is formed. The point here is that they did some things right to start with.

This chapter discusses a few of the "right" things to do in developing a youth ministry. The points discussed are meant to be examples of how to start, promote, and foster a group. The items mentioned are neither exhaustive nor complete. They simply represent the little items that pay big dividends, or the embellishments on the house called youth ministry.

Identifiable Image

As discussed earlier, two of the strongest needs of teens are the search for *identity* and the need to *belong*. These two items intersect at the point of youth ministry. The questions for a youth group and its members become, Who are we? and, How do I belong?

St. Paul's discovered one of the ways to speak to those questions. They invented a *name* for the group—SPY. The name gives the group a unique identity, and the youth belong to this group by adopting themselves to the group ("I am a member of SPY").

It may seem like such an insignificant thing, but a name becomes very important. It can become the identifying mark for the youth of a church. It becomes the focal point for publicity and promotion. Interest develops around it and the youth group creates an image with which they can identify themselves and feel a sense of belonging, and an image that the rest of the congregation identifies.

The name can be an anagram as in the case of St. Paul's Youth, or it could be a descriptive name, like the Seekers, Chosen Joy, or Fish. The name can even change over a period of years as the group changes, although this can cause confusion in congregational identity.

There are also many things that can be done with names to help create and promote the image of a group. A *logo* could be designed which could be used on stationery for the group or made into a banner representing the group.

Using either the name or the logo or both, T-shirts, hats, bumper stickers, or license plates can be made. It may sound somewhat childish, but watch what happens to a group that has a name and each person wears the identifying insignia of that group. The needs for identity and belonging are met, and the group develops cohesiveness because of it.

The only caution here is that the youth themselves must be in on the decision. If there was one point of question about St. Paul's approach, it was that the youth themselves did not help choose the name. Before any more decisions are made regarding a logo or identifiable objects (hats, T-shirts, buttons), the youth involved need to be included in the decision-making.

"What Is SPY?"

The question asked by Jack, Tom, and Martha before the vestry meeting of St. Paul's Church was: "What is SPY?" The question arose out of a bulletin announcement of the last Sunday. People were obviously curious. No doubt, there would be people scanning next Sunday's bulletin for further word. Interest was mounting; energy was going into discussing what this "thing" could be.

All of this serves as an example of something that is important in developing a youth program—*promotion*. This is different from publicity, which is meant to be an informative vehicle. Promotion means the stirring up of interest in an enterprise or endeavor. In youth ministry, it means keeping the name and activities before the congregation and all youth regularly. Promotion also connotes growth and development.

There are many ways to actively promote a good youth ministry. The weekly church bulletin is an excellent way. Every week there should be some statement about the youth group. It could be reporting something that was done or publicizing a future activity or event. If the group has an identifiable name, that name should always be used. A monthly newsletter done by the church is also a good avenue for promotion. Here is a chance to go into more detail. Use the names of the youth involved in various activities, report successful events, share learnings. In other words, tell who the group is and what it is about.

A church bulletin board designated especially for youth ministry is another opportunity for promotion. Make displays of activities, announce future events, take and mount pictures of past programs. Again, use the name of the group and any identifying logo as an attraction point to have people notice what and who the group is.

Area newspapers are still another way to promote the group. Small-town newspapers in particular are often looking for items of local news. Send them pictures and well written articles that promote what the group is doing.

These are simply examples of ways to do active promotion. There are two keys to doing good promotion: (1) consistency and (2) positiveness. Promotion needs to be done regularly and consistently. The name and activities of the youth group should be in front of people every time they pick up a piece of literature published by the church. This is an excellent way to demonstrate the ministry of youth. By means of articles in the bulletin and newsletter, the ministry of the church is shown to include the ministry of its youth. The other key is an attitude of positiveness. All promotion and publicity should be positive in focus. This is not the place to air dirty laundry. There is a big difference between reporting that "SPY gathered last Sunday to continue their shut-in gift project" and "Only six members of SPY were present last week for their meeting." The first example is not only good publicity for the project, it is also promotion for the group. A shut-in gift project is social ministry in action, and by reporting it, the group demonstrates that it *does* ministry for others. The second example, although probably overstated, has a somewhat negative tinge to it ("only six") and tells nothing about what has been or is being done. Regular promotion and positive attitude are very important factors. When promotion is done well, members of the group as well as members of the congregation will begin believing, "We have the best youth group around." That is not only a positive image to build, it becomes a goal to maintain.

Smoke Signals—And Other Forms of Publicity

Publicity is another important element in youth ministry. Whereas the goal of promotion is to stir up interest in the group, the purpose of publicity is to provide information about the activities of the group. However, well done publicity can also serve as good promotion.

The reason for publicity is to keep informed those persons who should know about or who are a part of the youth group. This can be done in numerous ways. All publications that are put out by a church should include items concerning youth news. Upcoming events and needed information can be publicized well in advance. A bulletin board for youth activities is another way. However, the most effective method of publicity is direct mail to the youth of the congregation. Since youth receive far less mail than adults, they are not as apt to discard it without opening it and reading the contents. Regular schedules of events can be sent out in this way, as well as reminder cards. The more creative and personal these cards and letters are, the better they work. Although it can be a costly venture, the payoffs can far exceed the costs in terms of active participation.

Good publicity really serves three functions. First, it keeps everyone informed. Second, publicity lets youth know that they are special, as a group and individually. If direct-mail publicity is used, youth feel a part of the ministry of this church. They feel special. They realize that someone knows they are around. As the group develops its own identity, publicity helps foster and promote that identity. The group develops a feeling about itself. They are special in the life of the church. They have a ministry to do and are part of the ministry of the church. Finally, good publicity is a form of encouragement for the youth and for the group. The identifiable image is kept alive. As a form of invitation, publicity serves as a way of encouraging those outside the group to become part of it. This is important as a group continues to grow, change, and expand.

A Few Little Extras

The house called youth ministry has been solidly built. Every facet of it has been covered. There remain a few items of philosophy about youth ministry that need to be taken into consideration. These are not meant as "gospel," but rather as observations based on experience.

1) The "numbers game" is a loser every time. The true concern in youth ministry should be the ministry done for, with, and by the youth. Unfortunately, many youth groups get overconcerned about the size of their group. They then begin to play what can be called the numbers game. The

object of the game becomes how large the group can get. The reason this is a loser is that the focus of the group becomes the number of people at any meeting or event rather than the ministry for, with, and by those who do come. This emphasis can lead to programming that is not balanced but that serves to attract the largest group. Youth ministry ceases being ministry when the diamond programming principle (chapter 5) is ignored or lost.

2) Develop a "can't quit" philosophy. Foster an openness that lets youth know they are always welcome. Once they come to a meeting or program, help them to feel a part of the group. Therefore, as a part, they can never quit. They may choose not to participate for awhile, but because they can't quit, the door is always open to them. One of the ways to express this attitude is to include all youth in the church who are youth-group age on the mailing list for publicity. By receiving regular mailings, a youth will soon begin to get the message of openness.

3) Do not underestimate the power of the sexes. One of the greatest drawing cards any group has is the members themselves. As youth search for intimacy (see chapter 3) in their lives, they begin to respond, react, and interact with members of the opposite sex. There is much energy that begins to get transferred between the sexes. It is important to be aware of this so that it can be used in healthy, constructive, growing ways for the youth and the group. This applies to everything from the sex ratio of the youth in the group to their actual activities and programs. Be aware of the dynamic and use it positively. Striving for a good sex ratio is one of the ways to do that.

4) Try to discover the appropriate night, times, and frequency for the group to gather. This can only happen in consultation with the youth themselves. In our pluralistic society, more and more time and energy demands are being made on youth. Youth ministry is meant to be supportive of

the youth as a growing person. Therefore, the intent for youth ministry is not to compete with other interests youth have nor to force the youth to make unnecessary choices regarding ultimate loyalty. In being supportive of and encouraging to youth, a good youth ministry program will seek to schedule its activities at times and with a frequency so as not to become another burden of responsibility for youth, but strives to be meaningful and fulfilling for them.

5) Pastoral involvement is usually a plus. The pastors who involve themselves in youth ministry are demonstrating their care and concern for the ministry of the youth of their parish. This involvement may be as simple as stopping by for a few minutes during meetings or as involved as being a part of the advisor team. The congregation also tends to look to the pastor as a leader. If he or she shows genuine interest in the youth and their program, he or she is being a good example for the rest of the congregation.

6) Underneath, beside, behind, above it all—there is prayer. Seek out guidance and help at its real source. The God of love and grace works wonders in and through us. Go to him as a group in prayer and discover his presence in the group. Let private prayer become a regular part of the youth program. Encourage the prayers of the congregation for the youth and their ministry. There is power and wisdom beyond human understanding available to the bowed head and folded hands.

"Where Do We Begin?"

After everything that has been said, the question that still needs to be asked is, "Where do we begin?" The answer is obvious:

1) Begin where one is. Take a good, hard look at the present situation. What needs to be done? What needs changing?

2) Learn the history of one's particular youth ministry.

109

What has been done in the past? What were the successes and failures?

3) Be creative. The best resource any group has is itself. Use the creative energy and ideas of the group to build.
4) Build patiently. Rome was not built in a day.
5) Pray. Let the Holy Spirit be an active partner in youth ministry.

Chapter Eight

A Trip on the Mountain —The Retreat

"I wonder how the youth are doing?" commented Mary Sims on her way into the church lounge where an adult Sunday church school class was about to begin.

"Oh, they're probably having a great time," June Linebaugh responded. "They seem to love those retreats. Where did they go this time?"

"I think they went to some retreat center. I know they went by bus and they left early in the morning," chimed in John Silva.

"But what do they do on these retreats?" Mary broke in. "They go on so many, it seems, and they always come back enthused and ready to go again."

"Well, last time my Denise went along," June offered. "When she came home she was exhausted. All she did was sleep for two days. Then when I asked her how the retreat was, all she said was, 'It was neat.' I still don't know all they did."

"As long as they enjoy themselves," added John, "that's all that matters."

One of the Winners

Obviously, the adults knew little about what went on at their church's youth retreats, but they did see the effects. Those effects were seen positively—"go on so many," "come back enthused," "ready to go again," "it was neat," "love those retreats."

Retreats can be among of the best building experiences any youth group uses. Over the years, they have become more and more popular, to the place where everyone and everybody goes on retreats. However, as is the case with any popular fad, retreats can lose their importance and significance if they are held just for the sake of having them. There is real value to *real* retreats, but as in all things, those retreats need to be built on a solid foundation.

Every group planning a retreat needs to begin with an understanding of the purpose for that retreat. Although the purpose will vary from group to group, all retreats have a threefold purpose:

1) To step back from the action. The word "retreat" itself means to go back, withdraw to a safe or private place. As the pressures of day-to-day living increase, everyone longs for a place and time of quiet repose. Retreats are meant to offer that place and time. It is a time of going away from the normal activities of daily living, to step out of the pace, to free oneself from the action.

2) To reflect intentionally. One does not find a hiding place simply to escape. Retreats offer the opportunity to do some serious reflection. It is a time of taking stock, of getting in touch, of intentional pause. This can become hard work but it is still one of the purposes for getting away. Refreshment and reflection go together in retreats.

3) To create community. As a group embarks on a retreat, one of the things they will discover is that they must learn to live together. Even if it is a silent retreat, where no one talks except briefly, the group must develop into a working, living community. This is not as easy as it sounds. It takes effort and planning to create this community, but that creation can be one of the richest rewards discovered on the retreat. A community of caring, loving, worshiping, working people is an enriching experience.

The purposes and goals of any retreat really depend on

what the group decides it needs and wants. However, the three purposes just stated are present to some degree in all retreats.

The questions may be asked: Why are retreats winners? What makes retreats so popular? Why do youth who go on them seem to come home both exhausted and enthused?

There are two answers to all those questions:

1) Retreats offer *depth*. Although retreating from the mainstream of everyday life, retreats provide an opportunity to delve deeply into issues or self. Depending upon the specific purpose of the retreat, those issues could be anything from Bible studies to topical issues to theological concepts to reflecting on self and where one is going. The depth is created because of the amount of time available, free from everyday chores and concerns, to do that kind of serious study. For instance, on a weekend retreat, a confirmation class can cover three months worth of material if they normally only meet one hour a week. That three months worth of material can be covered in a lot more depth and continuity than on a one-hour-a-week basis where much of the time is spent in review of what went on before.

2) Retreats provide *intensity*. Although retreats provide escape from normal activities, there is no escape from what happens at the retreat. Living together in a new environment offers its own set of problems. A group struggling to create a caring community will feel that intensity and will strive to live in it. This intensity is not a bad thing. It means everyone must work hard to care for and deal with one another. There is no escape from the retreat itself. This is why many persons who go on retreats come home both exhausted and enthused. They are exhausted because of the intensity of living with others in a new situation and of striving to create a community that can live together. They are enthused because the effort is generally a rewarding one where people learn about themselves and others.

113

Planning a Retreat

Retreats come in many styles, shapes, and forms. What happens at a retreat really depends on how it is planned. Too many groups go on what they call "retreats" without having planned what they are going to do. This is a good way to create boredom. It is the old question, "Well, what do you want to do now?" asked in a new setting. The results are the same.

As in all parts of youth ministry, intentional planning is always best. A retreat that is well planned does three things. First, a planned retreat makes the best use of time. If the whole group must decide what it's going to do next after each activity, over 50 percent of the time will be used in decision-making. Granted, decision-making is an important process to learn, but the best way to learn it is in structured circumstances that help persons reflect on what is happening. A retreat offers depth and intensity because of the time factor. There are only a certain number of days and hours to be used. Planning helps the participants to use that time wisely. Second, a planned retreat will build in balance in the program. The concern for a balanced program pervades all of youth ministry, and retreats are no exception. A retreat consisting entirely of recreation can easily become boring, as can a retreat of only small-group discussions. In accordance with the diamond principle for programming, a well-planned retreat will include recreation, worship, learning, and service events. Not all of the four areas need to be covered in proportion to the others, but something of each should be offered. Again, what is done depends on the purpose for the retreat. A retreat designed basically as a learning venture should also include some recreation and worship activities. Perhaps a service project that is appropriate to the material might also be done. Keeping a good balance of activities is important for retreats. Third, a theme should be developed. The theme should really reflect the purpose or the goal for the retreat. This means that everything that is done is a part of the theme.

The planning process outlined in chapter 5 works excellently when planning retreats. Here the group is concerned with a specific event in a given time period. If the planning process is new, why not try it on an activity that can be a winner—a retreat.

Where a group goes for a retreat depends on what they wish to do and what is available. A retreat can be held anywhere, as long as it is away from the everyday action of the people involved. Retreat centers, camps, and campgrounds offer excellent places. A retreat at another church can easily be arranged and is good fellowship, especially if the youth group of that other church joins the fun. Perhaps church members have cabins or summer homes in the mountains or at a shore or lake. Be creative and resourceful in planning where the group goes. Find out what is available and what is offered. However, remember that the facility does not make the retreat; good planning does.

ADDITIONAL RETREAT PLANNING TIPS
1) Use a good planning process which involves the young people in the planning.
2) Involve the youth in implementing the retreat—share the leadership.
3) Develop a retreat budget based on what is being planned.
4) Make a list of everything needed for the retreat and check each item off before leaving.
5) Have enough adult advisors to handle the size of the group and the activities planned.
6) Give detailed information to parents before the retreat. Let them know such things as: When leaving? When returning? What will the youth need to take? How much money will each youth need? Who are the advisors?

115

What is the phone number where the group can be reached? Who are the drivers?

7) Gather any medical information on allergies or other health problems or medication for the youth going.

8) Make sure there is some form of insurance coverage for the group. There are group policies available from independent insurance agents at nominal fees.

9) Leave the place where the retreat is held in as good shape as it was found.

10) Help youth to think through how they will relate what happened on the retreat when they are back home.

11) Deal with the problem of re-entry as the youth move back into their everyday lives.

12) Have fun.

Chapter Nine
"Help!" "S.O.S." "What Now?"
—Resources

One of the most constant cries heard in youth ministry is that of "Where do we go for help?" It is the cry of the adult advisor. The cry may take many forms: What can we do? What new programs can we try? Who or what can we turn to for ideas? What is available for us to use?

All these questions deal with *resources*. Any growing, creative youth ministry is always searching for new ideas to try, new events to do, new people to motivate the group. There are all kinds of resources available to any group. However, two words of advice about these resources are in order. First, it is important to remember that any resource is only as good as those who are using it. A new, fresh idea poorly planned and implemented still comes out as a poor program. A book full of programs is only good if those who are using that book know how to make those programs come alive for their group. Second, it is always important to remember that the best resource any group has is the members of the group themselves. Each person is unique and different. Each person brings talents and interests that are unique. The more diverse the group as to age, grade, and background, the richer the resources available. This is also true for advisors. The team concept provides more resources for a group to draw upon because it provides more involved people. No matter how good outside ideas may be, the best are always those dreamed up and built upon creatively by the group itself.

There are only three kinds of resources available to any group: people, things, and ideas.

1) *People*. As already stated, the best people resources are the people involved in a group themselves. However, there are other persons who serve as resources. Advisors are excellent resources. The pastor is a good resource for a group to tap. Find out what he or she thinks the group should or could be doing. Discover, through the pastor, where the youth can be involved in the ministry of the congregation. Have the pastor pass on to the youth council or advisors any mail that might be relevant to your ministry.

Most denominations also provide people resources to help congregations in their youth ministry. Find out from the pastor if there is someone on a churchwide level who can be a contact for help, information, or ideas for your group. Almost all denominations have someone functioning in the area of youth ministry. Find out who and what they have to offer.

2) *Things*. When people think of things as resources, they normally think of tools or equipment used to do a job. Without stretching the point too far, there are tools needed and helpful in youth ministry. Some of these tools have already been alluded to. The tools needed are really skills that help a person work with others and in a group. A list would include such skills as leadership, communication, listening, group development, motivation, program planning—and the list can go on and on.

Where does one acquire those skills? There are numerous workshops, conferences, training labs, and skill improvement events held all over the United States and Canada. Not all these events deal specifically with youth ministry skills, but what one learns in one situation can easily be translated into another area. There are also many workshop-type events available specifically designed for those in youth ministry. Have the pastor (who normally gets all the mail) forward any workshop publicity pieces to the appropriate persons in the group. Check also with the denominational headquarters to see what they are offering or know of that would be helpful in developing skills.

Films and plays are also excellent resources for youth ministry. Rental catalogs are available for films and filmstrips that deal with a variety of subjects. Check the resource bibliography at the end of this chapter for places to write for catalogs.

3) *Ideas.* Chapter 5 dealt with where ideas for programs can be acquired. The best suggestion for developing ideas is still the group members themselves as they brainstorm and build upon their own ideas. There are countless resource idea books available for any group.

A good idea for any group is to develop a "file" of ideas. Anyone who comes upon an idea can write it down or clip it out and put it into the file for future reference. An idea notebook could also be started. Jot down fresh ideas. A group that is on a constant search for new ideas will be one that has a fresh, creative ministry.

Resource Concepts

Adequate and relevant resources are a constant concern for those involved in positions of leadership in youth ministry. It used to be that people thought one resource book would solve all the problems. However, it never worked out that way because no one book or resource can meet all the needs of any one group.

Therefore, a group needs to be eclectic in its choosing of resources—drawing from many to try to meet the needs of its group and to keep a balanced overall program. All resources need to be selected with a given program and a specific group in mind. This is why a list of resources comes at the end of a book on creating a solid youth ministry. It is only after a group has discovered its need and concerns, using a good planning process, that they are ready to search for appropriate resources or tools to assist them in carrying out their program. The house must be built first before the activities can go on inside.

There are two concepts to keep in mind when using any

resource: (1) *Adapt*, do not adopt. Every program done by someone else or suggested by someone else is only applicable to another group as it is adapted, changed, altered to meet the needs and fit the purposes of that group. (2) *Create*, do not imitate. It is the same point in different words. Youth ministry is created, and that means that every group is different. It is in the creation that the real dynamic for youth ministry happens.

Youth Ministry Resource Bibliography

The listing that follows is by no means exhaustive. Relevant resources for youth ministry are numerous and easily located with some searching. Build a library of resources and be on a constant lookout for ideas that may be relevant to your situation.

DRAMA AND FILMS

AC1 Films, Inc., AC1 Productions, 35 West 45th Street, New York, NY 10036.

Audio-Visual Resource Guide. Friendship Press, 475 Riverside Drive, New York, NY 10027.

Association Films, Association Instructional Materials, 866 Third Avenue, New York, NY 10022.

Contemporary/McGraw-Hill Films, 330 West 42nd Street, New York, NY 10036.

Contemporary Drama Service, Box 547, 921 Curtiss Street, Downers Grove, IL 60515.

C.S.S. Publishing Company, 628 South Main Street, Lima, OH 45801.

The Eccentric Circle Cinema Workshop, P.O. Box 1481, Evanston, IL 60204.

Family Films and Filmstrips, 5823 Santa Monica Boulevard, Hollywood, CA 90038.

Films Incorporated, 1144 Wilmette Avenue, Wilmette, IL 60091.

Fortress Film Service, 2900 Queen Lane, Philadelphia, PA 19129.

Friendship Press, 475 Riverside Drive, New York, NY 10027.

Insight Films, Paulist Productions, P.O. Box 1057, Pacific Palisades, CA 90272.

Johnson-Nyguist Productions, 18414 Eddy Street, Northridge, CA 91324.

120

Learning Corporation of America (subsidiary of Columbia Pictures Industries, Inc.), 711 Fifth Avenue, New York, NY 10022.

Mass Media Industries, 2116 North Charles Street, Baltimore, MD 21218.

National Council of the Churches of Christ, Department of Church Culture, Offices of Publication and Distribution, 475 Riverside Drive, New York, NY 10027.

Pyramid Film Producers, Box 1048, Santa Monica, CA 90406.

"Short Plays," The Youth Ministry Leader's Library. Nido Qubein and Associates, Inc., P.O. Box 5367, High Point, NC 27262.

TeleKETICS (St. Francis Productions), 1229 South Santee Street, Los Angeles, CA 90015.

Time/Life Films, 43 West Sixteenth Street, New York, NY 10011.

United Church Press, 1505 Race Street, Philadelphia, PA 19102.

BOOKS AND MAGAZINES

Adventures with Youth. Nido Qubein and Associates, Inc., P.O. Box 5367, High Point, NC 27262.

Alive magazine. Christian Board of Publication, Box 179, St. Louis, MO 63166.

Christopher News Notes. 12 East Forty-Eighth Street, New York, NY 10017.

Clues to Creativity. Friendship Press Distribution Office, P.O. Box 37844, Cincinnati, OH 45237.

Discussion Starters for Youth Groups, Series 3, by Ann Billupo. Judson Press, Valley Forge, PA 19481.

Extend: Youth Reaching Youth, by Kenneth Fletcher, et al., 1974. Augsburg Publishing House, 426 South Fifth Street, Minneapolis, MN 55414.

The Five Cries of Youth, by Merton P. Strommen. Harper & Row Publishers, Inc., 10 East Fifty-Third Street, New York, NY 10022.

Fun and Festival Series. Friendship Press, 475 Riverside Drive, New York, NY 10027.

Fun Party Games, by Bernice Hagan, 1969. Hewitt House, Old Tappan, NJ.

Gaming, by Dennis Benson, 1976. Abingdon, 201 Eighth Avenue, S., Nashville, TN 37202.

Getting It Together in Youth Ministry, by Bill Ameiss, 1977. Lutheran Youth Encounter, Inc., 2500 39th Avenue NE, Minneapolis, MN 55421.

Group magazine. Thom Schultz Publications, P.O. Box 481, 118 East Fourth Street, Loveland, CO 80537.

121

Handbook of Co-Ed Teen Activities, by Edythe and David De Marche. Association Press, 291 Broadway, New York, NY.

A Handbook of Structured Experiences for Human Relations Training (6 vols.), ed. I. William Pfeiffer and John E. Gones. University Associates, Publishers and Consultants, 7596 Eado Avenue, La Jolla, CA 92037.

Heaven's-a-Poppin'. The Institute of Church Renewal, 1870 Tucker Industrial Blvd., Tucker, GA 30084.

How Persons Grow in a Christian Community, ed. Leonard A. Sibley. Philadelphia: Fortress Press, 1972.

Human Relations Reader, ed. John Denham, 1975. Mid-Atlantic Training Committee, Inc., Suite 325, 1500 Massachusetts Avenue, NW, Washington, DC 20005.

Is There Life After High School? by Ralph Keyes, 1976. Warner Books, Inc., 75 Rockefeller Plaza, New York, NY 10019.

The Junior Highs: A Manual for Youth Ministers, by Ginny Ward Holderness. St. Mary's Press, Christian Brothers Publications, Winona, MN 55987.

The Junior High Ministry, by Millie Greene. Reformed Church in America, 475 Riverside Drive, New York, NY 10027.

"Laugh and Grow" Games. Serendipity, P.O. Box 7661, Colorado Springs, CO 80933.

Learning With magazine. Division for Parish Services, 2900 Queen Lane, Philadelphia, PA 19129.

More-With-Less Cookbook, by Doris Janzen Longacre. Herald Press, Scottdale, PA 15683.

The New Games Book, New Games Foundation, P.O. Box 7901, San Francisco, CA 94120.

The New Generation and the New Creation, ed. Albert H. van den Heuvel, 1965. Friendship Press, 475 Riverside Drive, New York, NY 10027.

Organizing for Youth Ministry, by Charles Courtoy and Clifford E. Kolb, Jr., 1971. The Board of Discipleship, The United Methodist Church, Att: Division of Education, P.O. Box 840, Nashville, TN 37202.

Peer Program for Youth, by Ardyth Hebeisen, 1973. Augsburg Publishing House, 426 South Fifth Street, Minneapolis, MN 55414.

Power. Christian Youth Publications, 4466 West Pine 15 F, St. Louis, MO 63108.

Probe. Christian Association of Southwestern Pennsylvania, Department of Communications, 401 Wood Street, 1800 Arrott Building, Pittsburgh, PA 15219.

Program Planning for Youth Ministry, by John E. Forlite. St. Mary's Press, Christian Brothers Publications, Winona, MN 55987.

Respond books. Judson Press, Valley Forge, PA 19481:
    Respond, Vol. 1, ed. Keith L. Ignatius, 1971.
    Respond, Vol. 2, ed. Jan Corbett, 1972.
    Respond, Vol. 3, ed. Mason L. Brown, 1973.
    Respond, Vol. 4, ed. Barbara Middleton, 1975.

Retreat Handbook, by Virgil and Lynn Nelson. Judson Press, Valley Forge, PA 19481.

Serendipity books, by Lyman Coleman. Word, Inc., Waco, TX 76703:
    Acts Alive—creative expression
    Breaking Free—Christian liberation
    Celebration—Christian encounter
    Discovery—Christian community
    Kaleidoscope—Christian communication
    Man Alive—self-discovery
    Rap—personal life-style
    Serendipity—personal relationships
    Festival—filmmaking
    Beginnings—personal growth
    Groups in Action—mission outreach
    Coffee House Itch—coffee houses

Total Youth Ministry, by Maria Edwards. St. Mary's Press, Christian Brothers Publications, Winona, MN 55987.

Youth Interrobang. The Institute of Church Renewal, 1870 Tucker Industrial Blvd., Tucker, GA 30084.

Youth magazine. Room 1310, 1505 Race Street, Philadelphia, PA 19102.

The Youth Ministry Leader's Library. Nido Qubein and Associates, Inc., P.O. Box 5367, High Point, NC 27262.
    "Bible Studies"
    "Games"
    "Bible Quizzes"
    "Retreats"
    "Short Plays"

Youth Report. Grafton Publications, 331 Madison Avenue, New York, NY 10017.

Youth Worker's Success Manual, by Shirley E. Pollock, 1978. Abingdon, 201 Eighth Avenue, S., Nashville, TN 37202.

GENERAL RESOURCES (IDEAS, PROGRAMS, EVENTS)
    Alba House Communications, Canfield, OH 44406.

Argus Communications, 3005 North Ashland Avenue, Chicago, IL 60657.

Nido Qubein and Associates, Inc., P.O. Box 5367, High Point, NC 27262.

Saint Mary's Press, Christian Brothers Publications, Winona, MN 55987.

Son Power Youth Resources, Scripture Press Publications, Inc., 1825 College Avenue, Wheaton, IL 60187.

Young Life National Services, P.O. Box 520, Colorado Springs, CO 80901.

Youth Ministry Materials, P.O. Box 14325, St. Louis, MO 63118.

Youth Ministry Subscription Service, Division for Parish Services, 2900 Queen Lane, Philadelphia, PA 19129.

Youth Specialties, 861 Sixth Avenue, Suite 411, San Diego, CA 92101.

Notes

Chapter Two
1. Paul Johnson, "The Place of Children in the Church," *Learning With,* January 1979, p. 3.

Chapter Three
1. The complete report can be obtained by writing to the National Association of Secondary School Principals, 1904 Association Drive, Preston, VA 22091.
2. For copies of this report write for it by title, 1978 Youth Concerns Survey, to the Division for Parish Services, Lutheran Church in America, 2900 Queen Lane, Philadelphia, PA 19129.
3. Merton P. Strommen, *Five Cries of Youth* (New York: Harper, 1974), 155 pages.

Chapter Six
1. Merton P. Strommen, *Five Cries of Youth,* pp. 119-21.
2. *Ibid.,* p. 126.